D1517560

THE HISTORY OF THE
UNION PACIFIC
AMERICA'S GREAT
TRANSCONTINENTAL RAILROAD

RJM

THE HISTORY OF THE
UNION PACIFIC
AMERICA'S GREAT
TRANSCONTINENTAL RAILROAD

Edited by
Marie Cahill & Lynne Piade

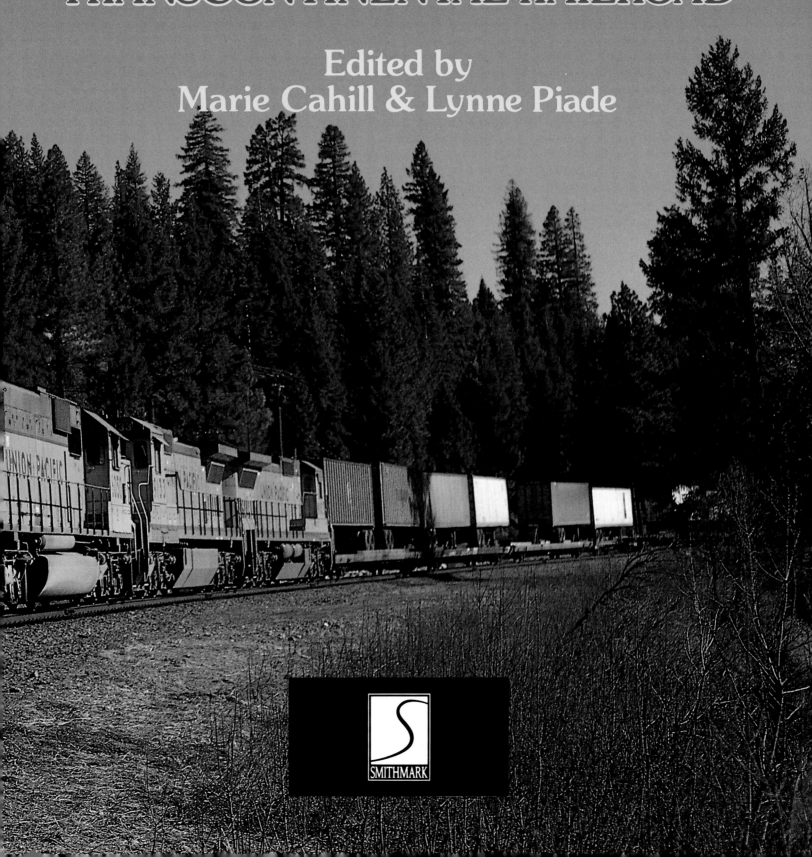

SMITHMARK

Copyright © 1989 Brompton Books Corp.

All rights reserved. No part of this publication may be reproduced, stored in a retrieval system or transmitted in any form by any means, electronic, mechanical, photocopying or otherwise, without first obtaining written permission of the copyright owner.

This edition published in 1994 by SMITHMARK Publishers Inc., 16 East 32nd Street New York, New York 10016

SMITHMARK books are available for bulk purchase for sales promotion and premium use. For details write or telephone the Manager of Special Sales, SMITHMARK Publishers Inc., 16 East 32nd Street, New York, NY 10016. (212) 532-6600.

Produced by Brompton Books Corp., 15 Sherwood Place Greenwich, CT 06830

ISBN 0-8317-3799-9

Printed in China

10 9 8 7 6 5 4 3 2

Designed by Ruth DeJauregui
Edited by Lynne Piade and Marie Cahill

Photo Credits
AGS Archives 6 (left), 10 (bottom), 26-27, 34, 37, 72, 78, 80, 100, 107 (left), 112 (left, upper right), 116, 118, 119 (lower left, right)
Amtrak 115
Association of American Railroads 16 (middle), 22-23, 25, 26, 30-31, 32, 49, 66 (left)
Bancroft Library 94-95
Bison Picture Library 59
DeGolyer Library, Southern Methodist University 82
© **RE DeJauregui** 4-5, 120, 122
Denver Public Library, Western History Department 86, 87
Georgia Department of Industry and Trade 112 (lower right)
General Motors Electro Motive Division 113
Nils Huxtable's Steamscenes 1, 2-3, 14-15, 42-43, 68-69, 73, 97, 101, 109, 117, 121, 124-125, 128
Library of Congress 20-21, 74, 75, 90-91
Montana Travel 112 (upper right)
National Railway Historical Society 38-39
Peter Newark's Western Americana 35, 65
Paul Orlow's Golden Spike Productions 51, 60, 70-71, 76-77, 79 (all), 103 (top), 110 (top, middle)
Pullman Company 67 (top)
Ron Ruhoff's Photomusical Adventures 62-63, 104-105, 113 (top), 127

Seaver Center for Western History Research, Los Angeles County Museum 84
Southern Pacific Railroad 16 (bottom, right), 17, 19, 50, 52, 81, 82-83, 89, 90, 92-93, 94 (inset), 98, 99, 102, 106, 107, 108 (top), 110 (bottom)
Texas State Library 48
Union Pacific Corporation 31 (top), 33 (right), 54-55, 56-57, 84-85, 111, 114 (bottom), 123 (all)
Union Pacific Museum Collection 9, 11, 12, 13, 16 (top), 21, 24-25, 28- 29, 33 (left), 34-35, 36, 40-41, 44-45, 52-53, 103 (bottom)
United States Department of Defense 108
Western Pacific Railroad Company 92,93, 119 (upper left)
Wyoming Travel Commission 7, 46-47
© **Bill Yenne** 6 (right), 10 (top)

Page 1: Now on display in Sacramento, the Union Pacific's steam engine 4466 evokes the days when steam ruled the rails.

Page 2-3: Dressed in its colors of blue and gold, UP's 6018 proudly winds its way through the forests of California.

These pages: Today, the Union Pacific refinery in Long Beach, California represents only a small segment of a large, diversified corporation that grew out of a dream to span the continent.

Contents

Introduction	6	The Harriman Era	88
Early History	8	The Early Twentieth Century	96
How We Built the Union Pacific	18	The Years Between the World Wars	100
Meeting at Promontory and After	50	World War II and Beyond	108
The Credit Mobilier Scandal	58	Mergers and Consolidations	116
The Golden Age of Railroading	64	The Union Pacific and the	
The UP Under Jay Gould	72	Railroad Industry Today	120
The Presidency of Charles Francis Adams, Jr	80		

Introduction

There are few railroads that evoke the legends of early American railroading as do those that were joined at Promontory, Utah by the epochal driving of the 'golden spike.' The Union Pacific formed the eastern portion of that historic union, and its story has grown with that of the United States itself. As the American frontier expanded across the continent, settlers bravely journeyed across the 'Great American Desert' in search of a better life on the West Coast. The journey was long and arduous, and the wagon trains that carried those first settlers across the nation inspired a vision of a great railroad spanning the continent. For the country to survive and prosper, its borders had to be linked, and thus was born the dream of the Union Pacific Railroad.

The promotion of an American transcontinental railroad, as it was then known, began in 1845, when the demand for goods from the Far East and exotic ports around the world inspired explorers and merchants to lobby Congress for funding to survey new routes to the Orient. By providing an alternate route, a transcontinental railroad would immensely reduce the time it took to sail around Cape Horn—the trip by sea took a hundred days or more whereas by train it would take just over a week. It would encourage settlement across the new territories in the West and would link California to the East Coast, thus serving as insurance against the state's secession from the Union.

Finally, all those aware of the developing North-South schism hoped that a Pacific railroad would make imminent their unification. War could not be averted, but when it was over, the nation again turned to its dream of a Pacific railroad to reunite the wartorn United States.

Theodore D Judah and Grenville M Dodge, both young engineers, charted rail routes through mountain passes, as they shared the dream of uniting California to the rest of the country. Judah drove through the Sierra Nevada, while Dodge found a path through the Black Hills at Lone Tree Creek. Their routes were to form the Pacific road one day. Whereas Judah didn't live to see the completion of the transcontinental road, Dodge lived to oversee the building of its eastern half, and not only saw its completion, but also witnessed the reorganization of the Union Pacific a quarter of a century later.

The sweat of many men went into the building of the nation's first transcontinental railroad, and when the final spike was driven home at Promontory the dream of a transcontinental railroad was realized; the event itself symbolized, to that generation, what landing on the moon would to a later generation.

Much has happened in the history of America's first transcontinental railroad. From the days of Grenville Dodge to the new expansions of the 1980s, which saw the UP widening its concerns to include waste management and pollution control, the history of the Union Pacific has been a long, but never uninteresting, progression toward the challenges of the future.

Below: **Major General Grenville M Dodge *(left)* and Theodore D Judah (right). Both men had the vision and determination to survey routes for a transcontinental railroad. Completed in 1887, the UP Depot at Cheyenne *(opposite)* was considered the finest depot along the line.**

Early History

Canals vs. Rails

When the young United States of America's overseas trade was disrupted by the outbreak of European wars in 1793, American leaders began to focus upon the abundant resources of their own continent's interior. As the frontier edged west—from the Appalachians to the Mississippi River—canals were built to facilitate trade with the nation's developing western frontiers. By 1825, canals were considered to be the most efficient form of transportation available. During the 1830s and 1840s, a fierce competition for trade developed between the transportation systems of the Mississippi and Ohio river valleys and the Erie Canal.

While most natural waterways flowed north to south, economic development was proceeding east to west. Privately financed by the state of New York, the Erie Canal, one of the few waterways that ran east-west, inspired railroad entrepreneurs to provide economical transportation that would compete successfully with water carriers. Moreover, canals were limited by the freezing winter weather and the Alleghenies. Thus, Congress saw in railroads the unimpaired ability to link the area east of the Allegheny Mountains with the West. The Baltimore & Ohio, the nation's first railroad, was chartered by the state of Maryland in 1827, and America entered an era of intense railroad building, all east of the Mississippi.

Great Britain had already proven the superior efficiency of wheels on rails over wheels on land. In an effort to find the best means of transportation, British entrepreneurs experimented with stationary engines used to haul a string of cars over the first set of 'rails'—wooden planks set on end. The first innovation on this system involved placing the engine itself on an additional car, supplying the power to the wheels and thereby moving the entire train, engine included. In 1829, George Stephenson showed the skeptics that his *Rocket* could pull a train of cars faster than a horse could pull a carriage. Railroads answered the limitations of canals and wagons, promising quicker, cheaper and more reliable service, and the canal building craze in the United States gave way to a rail building craze.

The Dream of a Pacific Railway

In 1842, the Webster-Ashburton Treaty defined a northwest boundary for the United States and created the Washington Territory. With this rich land now available to United States citizens and entrepreneurs, there was a growing demand for a railroad to the Pacific. The new territories of California, Nevada, Utah, Colorado, Wyoming, New Mexico and Arizona were acquired in 1848 after the War with Mexico, and their vast quantities of natural resources added to the growing expansionist excitement that prompted a host of legislation asking for a Pacific railroad. The discovery of gold in California and Colorado fueled the desire to move westward, as well as the need to find the fastest way there.

Like the fortune seekers of the frontier, many East Coast entrepreneurs embraced the idea of a transcontinental railroad. Since Caleb Cushing had secured the United States' first Far East trade agreement with China in 1844, the need for a more efficient China-East India trade route seemed pressing. This route would stretch from the United States' East Coast to its West Coast, rather than using the all-sea route around Cape Horn. Ten years later, Commodore Matthew Perry reached a trade agreement with the isolationist nation of Japan, thus furthering the necessity for a trade route across the country. New York tea merchant Asa Whitney, one of the many visionaries who foresaw a railroad spanning the continent, brought the proposal before Congress in 1850, but the majority of Congress did not approve of the project and no action was taken.

By the time Theodore Judah arrived in Washington, DC in late 1856 to lobby Congress for funding, the idea for a 'Pacific Railroad' had grown in popularity and was even seen by some as a national necessity. Judah, a civil engineer and builder of railroads, was one of the strongest advocates for such a transcontinental railroad. In 1860, during a trip across the country—via a sea route crossing the Isthmus of Panama—Judah persuaded Congressman-elect John Burch of California to introduce a transcontinental railroad bill to the House. Although the bill died in committee, it was then modified and revived as the Pacific Railroad Act of 1862, the first step in completing the Union Pacific Railroad. Judah was instrumental in its passage, and even received a testimonial from Congress praising his assistance in the act's passage. Ironically, Judah was associated with the Central Pacific, a rival of the Union Pacific.

Judah's counterpart at Union Pacific was Major General Grenville Mellon Dodge. Dodge, who was granted an indefinite leave from the Army, was named chief engineer for UP. It was these two who encouraged their respective employers, the 'Big Four' from Sacramento—Leland Stanford, Collis P Huntington, Charles Crocker and Mark Hopkins—who headed the Central Pacific, and Henry Farnam and Thomas C Durant from the Mississippi &

At right: **A poster urging residents of Great Britain to emigrate to the US. Many nineteenth century immigrants settled along the routes of the Union Pacific and Kansas Pacific, as the railroads had planned.**

THROUGH BOOKINGS

WITH THE

Glasgow and South Western

RAILWAY COMPANY.

THROUGH TICKETS

ARE NOW ISSUED TO LIVERPOOL IN CONNECTION WITH STEAMERS

TO THE STATES OF

KANSAS, NEBRASKA AND COLORADO.

CONNECTING WITH THE

UNION AND KANSAS PACIFIC RAILWAYS,

United States of America

These three States occupy a large region of country near the geographical centre of the American Union.

FARMING, STOCK RAISING, & MINING

Are the chief industries. Cheap and Fertile Lands are open for settlement in sufficient quantities to furnish Freehold Farms for all applicants. Extremely Healthy Climate, cheap Farming Implements, ample range for Live Stock, proximity to cash Markets east or west, superior Free Schools and Church privileges, the best social condition of society, and vast Mineral resources, offer unsurpassed opportunities for Tenant Farmers, their Sons and Families, as well as for Miners, Business Men, Labourers and their Families to better their condition, and all persons who intend removal to a new country should read all they can gather about these thrifty, growing states, which, as generally conceded, embrace

MANHATTAN ON KANSAS PACIFIC RAILWAY

SUMMIT LAKE, COLORADO

THE BEST COUNTRY NOW OPEN FOR SETTLEMENT.

The portions of the States to which attention is particularly invited are the sections traversed by the Union Pacific and Kansas Pacific Railways and their Branches. The population of the United States numbers at present about FIFTY MILLIONS, having increased about TEN MILLIONS since 1870.

NEBRASKA, KANSAS, AND COLORADO.

THE UNION PACIFIC, KANSAS PACIFIC, and CENTRAL BRANCH UNION PACIFIC RAILWAYS traverse the fertile, thrifty, and growing States of Kansas, Nebraska, and Colorado, the finest Agricultural and Stock-growing region in America. These Railway Companies have

SEVERAL MILLION Acres of unsurpassed Land for sale, in freehold farms, to suit the purchaser, at prices ranging from 8s. to £2 per acre, upon eleven years' credit, with a liberal discount for cash payments. These states offer superior inducements to settlers, as the immense mining operations in Colorado and other western states afford cash markets for their products in addition to the general cash markets at the east, and as they lie in the great highway of traffic through the central section of the United States they are becoming more rapidly settled, and property is more steadily advancing in value than any other portion of the American Union.

UPPER TWIN LAKE, COLORADO

PRAIRIE SCENE ON KANSAS PACIFIC RAILWAY

THE UNION PACIFIC, KANSAS PACIFIC, CENTRAL PACIFIC, and connecting Railways through the United States, form the line to the rich Mining Regions, and the Health and Pleasure Resorts of Colorado, Wyoming, Dakota, Montana, Idaho, Utah, Nevada, California and Oregon, and in connection with Steam Ship Lines on the Atlantic and Pacific Ocean form the most attractive route for travel and traffic to and from Europe and the Sandwich Islands, New Zealand, Australia, China, Japan, India, &c., all of which contribute to make the sections of country traversed by the Pacific Railways specially inviting to new settlers.

Full PARTICULARS of TRAIN SERVICE to LIVERPOOL can be obtained on application to the STATION MASTERS at any STATION on the

GLASGOW & SOUTH WESTERN RAILWAY,

and MAPS, PAMPHLETS, &c., can be obtained on

Application to Mr. P. B. GROAT, Gen. Agent for the Pacific Railways, Queen Anne Chambers, 1 & 2, Poultry, London, E.C., who will forward FREE valuable illustrated Books, Papers, Maps, and Circulars relating to this most interesting portion of the United States of America.

COLONIES. Special attention given to locating Colonies or parties of emigrants in Nebraska, Kansas or Colorado, and if desired, a personal visit will be made to any part of Great Britain to confer in relation to the formation of Colonies and removal of parties.

Address P. B. GROAT, Queen Anne Chambers, 1 & 2, Poultry, LONDON, E.C.

GRANT & CO. TURNMILL STREET LONDON E.C.

Missouri Railroad, representing the UP, to push on and make the dream of a Pacific railroad a reality. Later Durant and Farnam were on the Board of Directors of the Union Pacific.

The Controversy Surrounding Railroad Grants

At this time in American history, the government's role in the nation's economy was not well defined. Private enterprise believed in competition and a minimum of government intervention. When talk of federal grants in land or monetary aid to railroads circulated, many objected to it. Citizens in the Northeast regarded the land in the West as part of the public domain—and therefore under the control of the federal government. Opponents of the land grants could not see how such a large, isolated portion of public lands would benefit the country as a whole. The South opposed federal assistance, fearing that the government would favor the North in selecting a route.

Federal land grants to railroads followed extensive outlays for canal, river navigation and highway development.

Congress determined that railroads linking the Atlantic and Pacific Oceans were essential to national defense, development of the vast interior of the nation and improved trade. Because private investment in such an uncertain endeavor was not believed to be reliable, Congress provided federal land grants as an inducement to transcontinental railroad building, and was able to accomplish what had never been done before: provide transportation ahead of settlement. Despite the murmur of discontent by some, in 1850 President Millard Fillmore signed the first railroad land grants, more than 2.5 million acres, to the Illinois Central in Illinois and to the Mobile & Ohio in Mississippi and Alabama.

The land-grants program assisted almost all of the transcontinental railroads completed between 1862 and 1871—the Union Pacific and its branches, the Central Pacific, the Atchison, Topeka & Sante Fe, the Northern Pacific, the California & Oregon, the Atlantic & Pacific, and the Texas Pacific. The land-grant railroads more than repaid the value of their land-grant incentives—as affirmed by federal agencies, Congress and the Supreme Court. The Court also found that the sole obligation of land-grant railroads was merely to construct railroad lines; that the land grants represented prepayment for subsequent rail transportation of federal mail, troops and property; and that the railroads, by complying with conditions of their land grants, earned title to the lands. Clearly, railroad land grants were not gifts, but were earned compensation for the performance of a contract.

Turbulent Times

When President Abraham Lincoln signed the first Pacific Railroad Act in 1862, the United States was in the middle of a bitter, divisive debate. Animosities on both sides were excited by such explosive, controversial issues as slavery and states' rights. The South was threatening to secede and take California with it, while the North was afraid of losing California and thus also losing access to the potentially enormous wealth in the new western territories. In the midst of this turmoil, the dream of a Pacific railroad persisted.

The promise of fortune and power prompted a few determined men to take on the task of building a railroad two and one-half times the length of any railroad ever built. Easterners Peter A Dey and Doctor Thomas C Durant, and Westerners Charles Crocker, Collis Huntington, Mark Hopkins, and Leland Stanford were these determined men. Their transcontinental railroad, or Pacific railroad, as it was called, was potentially, as Lincoln and others hoped, the one joint venture that could unify the North and South.

"STEER" FOR THE IRON MOUNTAIN ROUTE

TO ARKANSAS, LOUISIANA, TEXAS, MEXICO AND CALIFORNIA

Many Southerners were opposed to the railroad. As of 1860 nearly two-thirds of all US railroads were in the North, and this was seen as a substantial advantage in the event of war. Railroads in the eleven Confederate states covered about 9000 miles, roughly one-third of the national rail mileage, but the average cost for the southern routes was two-thirds that of the average cost for the northern routes. The northern lines also had the advantage in power and rolling stock. Because the Confederacy had fewer production plants, it could not hope to equalize this disparity. The Civil War was the first American conflict in which railroads played an important part. General Sherman, a long-time promoter of railroads, cautioned, 'No army dependent on wagons can operate more than 100 miles from its base, because the teams going and coming consume the contents of their wagons.'

Opposite, left to right: **CP Huntington, Mark Hopkins, Leland Stanford and Charles Crocker—the Big Four. President Abraham Lincoln** *(far left)* **signed the Pacific Railroad acts.** *Above:* **The Iron Mountain Route was the origin of the Missouri Pacific, which today is part of the UP.**

Indeed, in two particular instances railroads played a major role in the military victories of the North over the South. The first involved a pincer movement on 2 June 1861, whereby the North secretly transported fresh troops by train and captured the town of Philippi, West Virginia, hoping to cripple the South. The North narrowly missed destroying the Southern forces stationed there because word of the surprise attack had gotten out. The second began as a raid and became a historic chase. In April of 1862, two civilians and eighteen Union soldiers stole the *General,* owned by the Western & Atlantic Railroad, from behind Confederate lines and headed north, planning to

burn bridges as they went in an attempt to destroy the Confederate supply link between Atlanta and the front at Chattanooga, Tennessee. The conductor, the engineer and a W&A foreman from the detached train gave chase at first on foot. They continued by push car and finally by commandeered locomotives, effectively deterring the raiders from doing serious damage. Just beyond Ringgold, Georgia the raiders abandoned the *General* and escaped capture.

Others were opposed to a Pacific railroad because, as a government chartered company, it would be subject to federal regulation despite being privately owned. This was felt to be a bad precedent by many businessmen. An objection that was raised by US senators was based on the fear of widespread corruption and a financial burden on the taxpayers that was seen as unfair. (Ironically, the scandal that would rock the railroad industry in 1872 occurred under the private management of Union Pacific official Doctor Durant, who, along with other UP officials, reaped $23 million in dividends from the false front construction company Credit Mobilier, and passed out its stock to influential members of Congress.)

Rather ironically, when the southern states seceded, Congress was free to act unfettered by the rivalry of northern and southern states over the proposed route. In 1862 the Pacific Railroad Act was signed into law. This act granted a charter to the Union Pacific Railroad Company. Land grants were also issued to the Central Pacific Railway of California, the Kansas Pacific Railway, the Sioux City & Pacific Railway and the Central Branch of the Union Pacific Railway. Each of these companies was allotted a 400-foot right of way and alternate sections within 10 miles of each side of the track, which was later increased to 20 miles, for

the construction of lines from the Missouri River to San Francisco. The Union Pacific would begin at Omaha, Nebraska and build west to Promontory, Utah, where it would connect with the Central Pacific, which had come from Sacramento, California under the management of Crocker, Huntington, Hopkins and Stanford, the Sacramento-based 'Big Four.' General John A Dix of New York City was the appointed president of the Union Pacific Railroad, but his involvement in army affairs kept him so busy that he passed his baton of leadership to his vice president, Dr Thomas C Durant.

The Gala

When the Union Pacific road crews reached the 100th meridian, 247 miles from Omaha, on 6 October 1866, a gala promotional was planned by Thomas C Durant—the doctor—and organized by Major General Grenville Dodge to supply their guests with three days of carefully orchestrated adventure and thrills in the wilds of the Nebraskan prairie. Late in October, two 4-4-0 American-type steam locomotives made their way west out of Omaha decorated with bunting and elk antlers affixed to the engine's headlights. These gay locomotives were pulling new Pullman Palace Sleeping Cars, filled with Union Pacific employees, provisions, bedding, tents, buffalo robes, wood for bonfires, cases of champagne, dignitaries, their wives and servants, three government commissioners, reporters, a photographer, an army of Union Pacific directors, caterers, barbers, and a band from St Joseph. Totalling 140, the guest list glittered with senators, congressmen, capitalists and other famous persons useful to the road. After all, this celebration was the perfect advertising campaign and the railroad

always needed backers. Durant capitalized on the aspect of self-mockery in selling the West.

The guests camped at Columbus the first night. There, a great circle was organized, and in the center Dodge lit a huge conflagration, awing the visitors with its brightness and initiating them in the ways of the campfire. The next day, some of the guests were escorted to the head of the line to watch the men at work laying track in a steady rhythm long familiar to railroaders. Other visitors observed a prairie dog colony not far from their camp; still others went hunting for the indigenous buffalo and fleet-footed antelope. In the evening a feast of game was prepared and the champagne flowed without restraint.Suddenly, without warning, Indian war cries rang through the still morning air. As they raced through the camp in full war paint and battle gear, the ladies screamed and the men peeped out of their tents at the spectacle. Dodge arrived on the scene and assured them that the invaders were really friendly Pawnees, some of whom had served as scouts and soldiers under him. Once the guests were calmed and dressed, the Pawnees demonstrated war dances and staged a mock battle featuring a scalping. The guests were measurably impressed and threw small coins to the performers and chatted with those who spoke English.

On the last night Durant planned a controlled burning of some prairie grass and at a safe distance the guests marvelled at the sight of the blaze. They had experienced the real Wild West and everyone left feeling satisfied. Durant was overjoyed that the extravaganza had gone so well. Despite his rather steep outlay costs, he concluded that 'From a sight-seeing point of view, it may be considered as very successful;' and resolved to stage promotional excursions any time the Union Pacific had an event to celebrate.

At left: **The golden spike ceremony, celebrating the meeting of the UP and Central Pacific at Promontory on 10 May 1869.** *The overleaf* **shows a recreation of this historic event.** *Above:* **Samuel Montague of the CP** *(left)* **and Grenville Dodge of the UP** *(right)* **exchange congratulations.**

The Golden Spike

When the Union Pacific reached Promontory on 10 May 1869, the company celebrated once again. Durant, his two great engineers, Peter A Dey and Grenville M Dodge, and the track-laying contractors, Jack and Dan Casement, were on board the Union Pacific's Number 119 locomotive chosen for the special occasion. Likewise, from the west came Central Pacific's *Jupiter* locomotive, bearing then Governor Leland Stanford, representing the Big Four, three of whom didn't show. The two locomotives had several notable differences. UP's Number 119, a coal-burner, stood staight and tall in contrast to the *Jupiter's* rounded balloon stack. The Union Pacific, dressed in dark green and black, was somber, whereas the *Jupiter* was brightly dressed in vivid scarlet. Both, however, were decked out with gleaming brasswork.

About noon, Grenville Dodge stepped forward and asked for silence. A laurel tie was placed on the grade, followed by the last two rails, and finally the golden spike was put in place, to be driven home by the dignitaries of each side. Unfortunately, neither Durant nor Stanford could muster the strength or the accuracy to drive the spike home, and the final blows were given by those most worthy: chief engineer Grenville M Dodge and Dan Casement for the Union Pacific, and Samuel S Montague of the Central Pacific. There are conflicting reports as to who hammered in the spike last, but all agree that none of the officials were competent at tracklaying and even the telegrapher, WN

Shilling, flashed 'Done' before it was actually in the railroad tie because his view was blocked and he assumed that it had been accomplished by the officials.

As the blows of the hammer were being transmitted by telegraph throughout the entire Western Union system, the nation was celebrating. New York fired a hundred-gun salute, Philadelphia rang the Liberty Bell, Chicago decorated itself in bunting, and San Francisco set off the cannons at Fort Point.

The famous golden spike ceremony at Promontory, Utah, near Ogden, marked the culmination of the construction of the nation's first transcontinental railroad. Later, the Central Pacific (now part of the Southern Pacific line) would build west from Sacramento to the Western Pacific Railroad, while the Western Pacific would build from San Jose to Sacramento. By 1869, the entire line from Omaha to San Jose was completed. The Kansas Pacific was entrusted to build from Kansas City to junction with the Union Pacific in Nebraska, then westward to Denver, and then to make a final push north to form a junction with the Union Pacific in Cheyenne, Wyoming. The Sioux City & Pacific would connect with the Union Pacific at Fremont, Nebraska and later become part of the Chicago & Northwestern. The Central Branch of the Union Pacific would build the 100 miles from Atchison to Waterville, Kansas, a line now part of the Missouri Pacific.

Right: **A poster for the newly completed transcontinental railroad.** *Below:* **Side views of the golden spike, inscribed with the names of the two railroads' officers. Note that the spike at bottom bears the date 8 May 1869—the UP was two days late.** *Far right:* **A top view of the golden spike.**

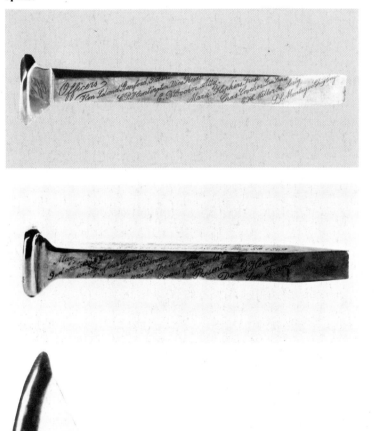

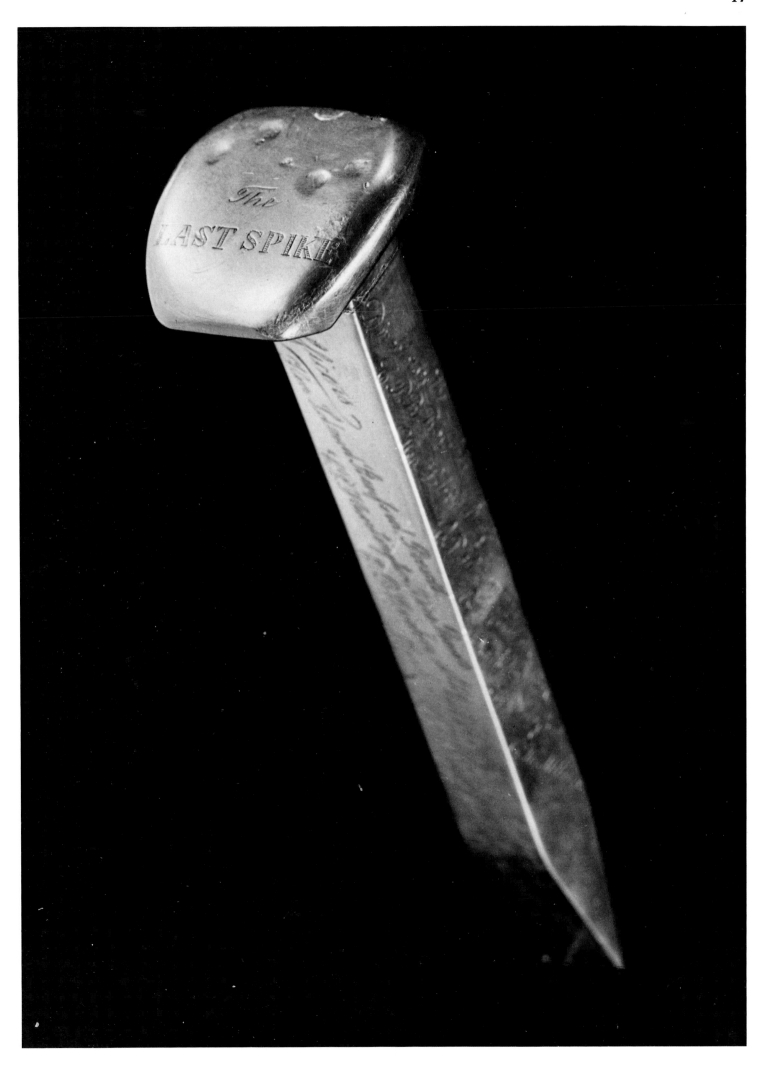

How We Built the Union Pacific

By Grenville M Dodge

Surveying the Route

In 1836, the first public meeting to consider the project of a Pacific railroad was called by John Plumbe, a civil engineer of Dubuque, Iowa. Interest in a Pacific railroad increased from this time. The explorations of Fremont in 1842 and 1846 brought the attention of Congress, and AC Whitney was zealous and efficient in the cause from 1840 to 1850. The first practical measure was Senator Salmon P Chase's bill, making an appropriation for the explorations of different routes for a Pacific railroad in 1853. Numerous bills were introduced in Congress between 1852 and 1860, granting subsidies and lands, and some of them appropriating as large a sum as $96 milion for the construction of the road. One of these bills passed one of the houses of Congress.

The results of the exploration ordered by Congress were printed in 11 large volumes, covering the country between the thirty-second parallel of latitude on the south and forty-ninth on the north, and demonstrating the feasibility of building a Pacific railroad, but at a cost (on any one of the lines) much larger than the Union Pacific and Central Pacific were built for. It is a singular fact that from all these explorations, the most feasible line from an engineering and commercial point of view, the line with the least obstacles to overcome, of lowest grades and least curvature, was never explored and reported on. Private enterprise explored and developed that line along the forty-second parallel of latitude.

This route was made by the buffalo, next used by the Indians, then by the fur traders, next by the Mormons, and then by the overland immigration to California and Oregon. It was known as the Great Platte Valley Route. On this trail, or close to it, was built the Union and Central Pacific railroads to California, and the Oregon Short Line branch of the Union Pacific to Oregon.

In 1852, the Mississippi & Missouri Railroad Company was organized to build a line westward across the state of Iowa as an extension of the Chicago & Rock Island, then terminating at Rock Island, Illinois. The principal men connected with this line were Henry Farnam and Thomas C Durant. Peter A Dey, who had been a division engineer of the Rock Island, was the chief engineer of the M & M in Iowa. He was a man of great ability, probity and integrity.

In May of 1853, Mr Peter A Dey left the Rock Island, of which he was a division engineer stationed at Tiskilwa, and commenced, at Davenport, Iowa, the first survey of a railroad line across the state of Iowa. I had been with Mr Dey about eight months as rodman, and under his direction had made a survey of the Peoria & Bureau Valley Railway in Illinois. Mr Dey was made chief engineer of the M & M, and took me to Iowa as his assistant, and placed me in charge of the party in the field—certainly a very fine promotion for the limited experience I had—and it is one of the greatest satisfactions and pleasures of my life to have had his friendship from the time I entered his service until now. Mr Dey is not only a very distinguished citizen of Iowa, but is one of the most eminent engineers of the country. He was known for his great ability, his uprightness, and the square deal he gave everyone, and he has greatly honored his state in the many public positions he has held. I look back upon my services with him with the greatest pleasure. He has a wide reputation as a civil engineer and railroad constructor, and in later years as railroad commissioner for the state of Iowa.

In 1853, he gave the orders for the party that surveyed the first line across Iowa to examine the country west of the Missouri River. This was to determine where the M & M (now the Rock Island) line crossing Iowa should terminate on the Missouri River, in order to take advantage of, and, perhaps, become a part of the prospective line running west up the Great Platte Valley, then the chief thoroughfare for all the Mormon, California and Oregon overland immigration. It fell to my lot to be chief of this party. My examinations

At right: Railroad veteran Amos L Bowsher (center) recalls, for his cronies, the historic day the golden spike was driven home at Promontory, Utah to complete the first transcontinental railroad.

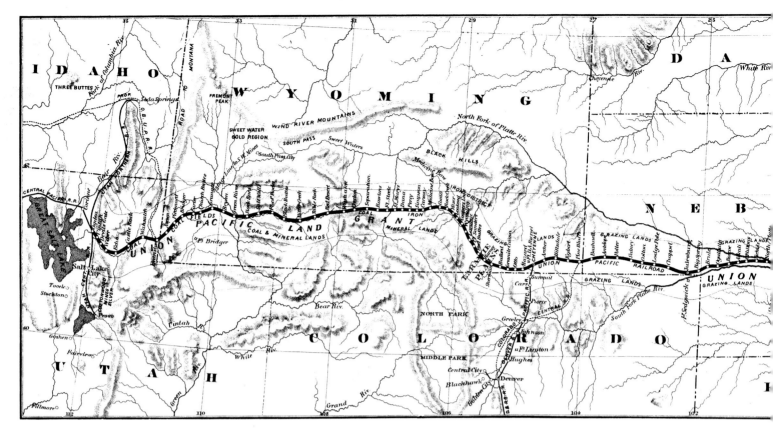

virtually determined that a railroad line extending west from the Missouri River should go by way of Sarpys Point (now Bellevue), or directly west from Kanesville, afterwards Council Bluffs, where the Mormons from Nauvoo were then resting on their way to Salt Lake.

My party crossed the Missouri River in the fall of 1853 on flatboats. The Omaha Indians occupied the country where we landed, and after obtaining a line rising from the bluffs west of where the city of Omaha now stands, I gave directions to the party to continue the survey, while I went on ahead to examine the country to the Platte Valley, some 25 miles farther west. I reached the Platte Valley about noon the next day, and being very tired, I lariated my horse and laid down with my saddle as a pillow and with my rifle under it, and went sound asleep.

I was awakened by the neighing of the horse, and when I looked up I saw an Indian leading the horse toward the Elkhorn River, pulling with all his might and the horse holding back, evidently frightened. I was greatly frightened myself, hardly knowing what to do, but I suppose from instinct I grabbed my rifle and started after the Indian, hollering at the top of my voice. The Indian saw me coming, let the horse go, and made his way across the Elkhorn River.

This Indian afterwards was an enlisted man in the battalion of Pawnees that served under me in the Indian campaigns of 1865, and he told Major North, the commander of that battalion, that he let loose of the horse because I hollered so loud that it frightened him. On obtaining my horse, I saddled up and made my way back to the party that was camped on the Big Papillion on the emigrant road leading from Florence to the Elkhorn. The camp was full of Omaha Indians and they had every man in the party cooking for them. I saw that we would soon lose all our provisions, and as the party was armed, I called them together and told them to get their arms. I only knew one Indian word, 'Puckechee,' which meant get out.

That I told them, and while the Indians were surly they saw we were determined and they left us. I don't believe there was anyone in the party that had ever seen an Indian before or had any experience with them. We were all tenderfeet. It taught me a lesson, never to allow an Indian in my camp or around it without permission, and these were my instructions to all our engineering parties. Those who obeyed it generally got through without losing their stock or lives. Those who were careless and disobeyed generally lost their stock and some of their men.

As soon as we had determined the line from the Missouri River to the Platte we returned to Iowa City, which was the headquarters of the M & M Railway. The times were such that the work on the M & M Railway was suspended for some years. Meanwhile, I located at Council Bluffs, continuing the explorations under the direction of Messrs Farnam and Durant, and obtaining from voyagers, immigrants and others all the information I could in regard to the country farther west.

There was keen competition at that time for the control of the vast immigration crossing the plains, and Kansas City, Fort Leavenworth (then the government post), St Joseph and Council Bluffs were points of concentration on the Missouri. The trails from all the points converged in the Platte Valley at or near old Fort Kearney, following its waters to the South Pass. A portion of the 'Kane City' immigration followed the valley of the Arkansas west, and thence through New Mexico. The great bulk of the immigration was finally concentrated at Council Bluffs, as this was the best crossing of the Missouri River.

From my explorations and the information I had obtained with the aid of the Mormons and others, I mapped and made an itinerary of a line from Council Bluffs through to Utah, California and Oregon, giving the camping places for each night, and showing where wood, water and fords of streams could be found. Distributed and broadcast by the local interests along this route, this map and itinerary had no small influence in turning the mass of overland immigration to Council Bluffs, where it crossed the Missouri and took the great Platte Valley route.

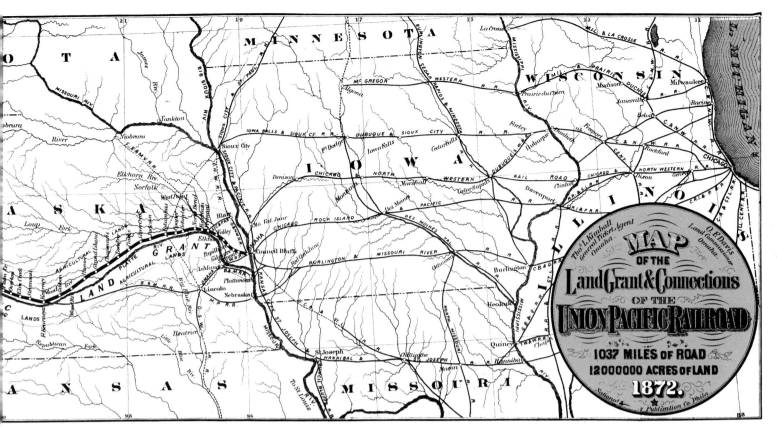

Above: A map of the Union Pacific line from Council Bluffs, Iowa to Ogden, Utah. *Below:* A poster, printed in March 1867, announced the shortest and quickest route across the country—via the Union Pacific.

This route was up that valley to its forks, and then up either the north or south fork to Salt Lake and California by way of the Humboldt, and to Oregon by way of the Snake and Columbia rivers. This is today the route of the Union and Central Pacific to California, and the Union Pacific route to Oregon.

After collecting all the information we could as to the best route for a railroad to the Pacific, I reported to Messrs Farnam and Durant, who paid out of their private funds for all my work. In 1857 or 1858, they asked me to visit New York. In the office of the Rock Island Railroad, over the Corn Exchange Bank on William Street, I was brought before the Board of Directors of that railroad and the Mississippi & Missouri Railway, together with some friends who had been called in.

The secretary of the company read my report. Before he was half through, nearly every person had left the room, and when he had finished only Mr Farnam, Mr Durant, the reader and myself were present. I could see that there was lack of faith and even interest in the matter. One of the directors said in the outer room that he did not see why they should be asked to hear such nonsense, but Messrs Farnam and Durant did not lose faith. Since our survey in 1853, other companies had made surveys in Iowa, all concentrating at Council Bluffs. Farnam and Durant felt that if they could stimulate interest in the Pacific road, it would enable them to raise funds to complete their line across the state, and authority was conferred upon me to begin work at Council Bluffs and build east through Pottawattamie County, if I could obtain local aid. This we secured, and the road was graded through that county, when we were called east to continue the work from Iowa City west.

In 1854, when Nebraska was organized, we moved to its frontier, continuing the explorations under the patronage of Messrs Farnam and Durant, and obtaining all valuable information, which was used to concentrate the influence of the different railroads east and west of Chicago to the support of the forty-second parallel line.

The Railroad Act of 1862

In 1861, we discontinued the railroad work because of the Civil War. The passage of the Act of 1862, which made the building of a transcontinental railroad possible, was due primarily to the persistent efforts of the Honorable Samuel R Curtis, a Representative in Congress from Iowa, who reported the bill before entering the Union service in 1861. It was then taken up by the Honorable James Harlan, of Iowa, who succeeded in obtaining its passage in March of 1862.

Up to 1858, all the projects for building a railroad across the continent were regarded as the 'Pacific roads,' each route mentioned having a particular name. The line along the forty-second parallel of latitude was designated as a line from San Francisco to a point on the Missouri River not farther north than Council Bluffs and not farther south than Independence, Missouri, and was called the Pacific Railroad. The line surveyed by Stephens along the forty-ninth parallel of latitude was called the North Route. The route along the thirty-eighth and thirty-ninth parallels was called the Buffalo Trail. It received that name from Thomas H Benton. The route along the thirty-fifth and thirty-second parallel was called the South Route.

The government, however, made no explorations along the forty-second parallel; that was done by individual enterprise. In 1856, both political parties, in convention, passed resolutions favoring a Pacific railroad, and in 1857 President Buchanan advocated it as a reason for holding the Pacific coast people in the Union, and it was this sentiment that gave to the forty-second parallel line the name of the Union Pacific Railroad.

In 1858, a select committee of 15 on Pacific railroads was authorized by Congress and in the Thirty-fifth Congress, second session, this committee allowed the Honorable Samuel R Curtis, of Iowa, to report the bill, and if I recollect rightly, this was the first bill that took the name of Union Pacific.

In the Thirty-sixth Congress, General Curtis became the champion of the Union Pacific Railroad, and it was again advocated as a strong element in holding the Union together. Curtis's bill passed the House in December of 1860. It failed to become a law, as the question of secession was up then and Lincoln had been elected President. In the extra session of the Thirty-second Congress in July of 1861, Curtis reintroduced the bill and he left Congress to enter the army. Then Representative Campbell, of Pennsylvania, became chairman of the committee.

Senator Harlan, of Iowa, who had been elected to the Senate, became the strongest advocate of the bill in the Senate. Lincoln advocated its passage and building, not only as a military necessity, but also as a means of holding the Pacific coast to the Union. This bill became a law in 1862.

The Union Pacific Railway was organized on 2 September 1862 at Chicago, Major General SH Curtis, of Iowa, being chairman of the commissioners appointed by Congress. The organization was perfected by making Henry B Oden, of Chicago, President; Thomas W Olcott, Treasurer; and Henry V Poor, Secretary. Mr TC Durant selected Peter A Dey to make a reconnaissance from the Missouri River to Salt Lake to be reported at the next meeting of the board.

At left: A Hollywood depiction of a construction crew hard at work laying tracks for the transcontinental railroad as the 'Iron Horse' headed west to tame the wild frontier.

Mr Dey immediately entered upon his work and extended his reconnaissance through to Salt Lake Valley.

In the spring of 1863, when in command of the district of Corinth, Mississippi, I received a dispatch from General Grant to proceed to Washington and report to President Lincoln. No explanation coming with the dispatch, and having a short time before organized and armed some Negroes for the purpose of guarding a contraband camp which we had at Corinth—which act had been greatly criticized in the army and by civilians—I was somewhat alarmed, thinking that possibly I was to be called to account. But on arriving at Washington, I discovered that my summons was due to an interview between Mr Lincoln and myself at Council Bluffs back in August of 1859. He had been there to look after an interest in the Riddle tract he had bought from Mr NB Judd, of Chicago. I had just arrived from an exploring trip to the West. It was quite an event for an exploring party to reach the States, and after dinner, while I was resting on the stoop of the Pacific House, Mr Lincoln sat down beside me, and by his kindly ways soon drew from me all I knew of the country west, and the results of my reconnaissance. As the saying is, he completely 'shelled my woods,' getting all the secrets that were later to go to my employers.

Under the law of 1862, the President was to fix the eastern terminus of the Union Pacific Railway, and, remembering our talk in the 'fifties,' he wished to consult me in the matter. Several towns on the Missouri River were competing for the terminus, but Mr Lincoln practically settled the question in favor of the location I recommended. He issued his first order on 17 November 1863. It was in his own language, and as follows:

'I, Abraham Lincoln, President of the United States, do hereby fix so much of the western boundary of the State of Iowa as lies between the north and south boundaries of the United States township within which the city of Omaha is situated as the point from which the line of railroad and telegraph in that section mentioned shall be constructed.'

This order was not considered definite enough by the company, and on 7 March 1864, President Lincoln issued the second executive order, as follows:

'I, Abraham Lincoln, President of the United States, do, upon the application of said company, designate and establish such first-named point on the eastern boundary of

Below: Adorned with antlers, McQueen Engine Number 23 (built by Schenectady Locomotive Works in 1868) pauses at a Wyoming Station 15 miles west of Laramie. *At right:* Locomotive Number 5 and the UP's photography car near Point of Rocks, Wyoming in 1868.

the State of Iowa east of and opposite to the east line of section 10, in township 15 south, of range 13 east, of the sixth principal meridian in the Territory of Nebraska.'

On 8 March 1864, he notified the United States Senate that on the 17th day of November, 1863, he had located the 'eastern terminus of the Union Pacific Railway within the limits of the township in Iowa opposite to the town of Omaha. Since then, the company has represented to me that upon additional survey made it has determined upon the precise point of departure of the branch road from the Missouri River, and located same within the limits designated in the order of November last.'

He was very anxious that the road should be built and discussed that question with me.

I explained to him as clearly as I could how difficult it would be to build it by private enterprise, and said I thought it should be taken up and built by the government. He objected to this, saying the government would give the project all possible aid and support, but could not build the road; that it had all it could possibly handle in the conflict now going on. But the government would make any change in the law or give any reasonable aid to insure the building of the road by private enterprise.

After my interview with the President, I proceeded to New York and met Mr TC Durant, then practically at the head of the Union Pacific interests, and other interested persons. After I had presented the President's views they took new courage, and at the yearly meeting of the company General John A Dix was made President; Thomas C Durant, Vice President; HV Poor, Secretary; and JJ Cisco, Treasurer. They then submitted to Congress the necessary changes needed in the law of 1862, in order to bring the capital of the country to their support.

In the fall of 1863, Mr Durant had personally instructed Mr Dey to organize parties for immediate surveys to determine the line from the Missouri River up the Platte Valley, to run a line over the first range of mountains, known as the Black Hills, and to examine the Wasatch Range. In his report Mr Durant said:

'It is here that the information derived from the examinations made by General GM Dodge, and those made

Below: A grading crew at the Narrows at Weber Canyon, Utah—one of the most difficult stretches to grade. *At right:* Excited passengers wave to passers-by as the UP pulls into town—as portrayed by Hollywood.

last year by Peter A Dey, who was sent out by the committee appointed by your board of commissioners, proved of great value, as the present parties will avail themselves of the examinations made by these gentlemen, and will first run the lines which they found most practicable.'

In accordance with these instructions, Mr Dey placed BB Brayton in charge of the party examining the Black Hills, and, at Mr Dey's request, Brigham Young placed his son, James A Young, in charge of the surveys over the Wasatch. Mr Dey, who had become chief engineer, placed engineering parties in the field covering the territory from the Missouri River to Salt Lake.

Ground was broken at Omaha for the beginning of the road on the 1st day of December, 1863, and after the passage of the Act of 1864, about $500,000 was spent for grading and surveys.

A question as to the location brought a disturbing contest between Omaha and the company. Mr Dey had located the line due west to the Elkhorn River. The consulting engineer, Colonel Seymour, recommended a change, increasing the distance nine or more miles in 13. The main argument for adding miles of distance in 13 miles of road was that it eliminated the 80- and 66-foot grades of the direct line. If this had been done, there would have been some argument for the change; but they eliminated only the grades from the Omaha summit west, while it took three miles of 60- and 66-foot grade from the Missouri River to reach this summit, and coming east, the Elkhorn summit was an 80-foot grade, so by the change and addition of nine miles they made no reductions in the original maximum grades, or in the tonnage hauled in a train on the new lines over the old line, if it had been built. (The grades at Omaha and Elkhorn have been eliminated since 1900, and the new management is adopting the old Dey line for the distance it saves, and bringing the grade to the road's maximum of 47 feet to the mile).

It was Mr Dey's intention that when traffic demanded, the original short line grades would be reduced to whatever maximum grade the road should finally adopt. After a long contest and many reports, the government provided that the change should be made only if the Omaha and Elkhorn grades were eliminated—the first by a line running south from Omaha two miles down the Missouri Valley and cutting through the bluffs to Muddy Creek, giving a 35-foot maximum grade, and the Elkhorn by additional cutting and filling without changing the line, but this was never done.

The company paid no attention to the decision, but built on the changed line, letting the grades at Omaha and Elkhorn stand, and the government commissioners accepted the road, ignoring the government's conditions for the change, and bonds were issued upon it, although it was a direct violation of the government order. The final decision in favor of the change and the ignoring of Mr Dey's recommendations in letting the construction contracts caused Mr Dey, in January of 1865, to send in his resignation. He stated in his letter of resignation that he was giving up 'the best position in his profession this country has offered to any man.'

The officers of the Union Pacific then requested me to return and take charge of the work. I was then in command of the United States forces on the plains in the Indian

At left: **This steam shovel was needed to excavate the mountainous terrain at Hanging Rock in Echo Canyon, Utah during the building of the Union Pacific Railroad.**

campaigns, and General Grant was not willing that I should leave, so I finished my work there and went to Omaha on the first of May, 1866, and assumed the duties of chief engineer, having been allowed leave of absence through the following letter of Major General William Tecumseh Sherman:

HEADQUARTERS, MILITARY DIVISION OF THE MISSISSIPPI St Louis, 1 May 1866.

Dear General: I have your letter of April 27, and I readily consent to what you ask. I think General Pope should be at Leavenworth before you leave, and I expected he would be at Leavenworth by May 1, but he has not yet come. As soon as he reaches Leavenworth, or St Louis even, I consent to your going to Omaha to begin what, I trust, will be the real beginning of the great road. I start tomorrow for Riley, whence I will cross over to Kearney land, and thence come in to Omaha, where I hope to meet you. I will send your letter this morning to Pope's office and indorse your request that a telegraph message be sent to General Pope to the effect that he is wanted at Leavenworth. Hoping to meet you soon, I am,

Yours truly,
WT Sherman, MG

Construction Begins

The organization for work on the plains, away from civilization, was as follows. Each of our surveying parties consisted of a chief, who was an experienced engineer; two assistants, also civil engineers; rodmen, flagmen and chainmen, generally graduated civil engineers but without personal experience in the field; and axmen, teamsters and herders. When the party was expected to live upon the game of the country a hunter was added.

Each party would thus consist of from 18 to 22 men, all armed. When operating in hostile Indian country they were regularly drilled, though after the Civil War this was unnecessary, as most of them had been in the Army. Each party entering a country occupied by hostile Indians was generally furnished with a military escort of from 10 men to a company under a competent officer.

The duty of this escort was to protect the party when in camp. In the field, the escort usually occupied prominent hills commanding the territory in which the work was to be done, so as to head off sudden attacks by the Indians. Notwithstanding this protection, the parties were often attacked, their chief or some of their men killed or wounded, and their stock run off.

In preliminary surveys in the open country, a party could run from eight to twelve miles of line in a day. On location in an open country three or four miles would be covered, but in a mountainous country generally not more than a mile. All hands worked from daylight to dark, the country being reconnoitered ahead of them by the chief, who indicated the streams to follow, and the controlling points in summits and river crossings. The party of location that followed the preliminary surveys had the maps and profiles of the line selected for location, and devoted its energies to obtaining a line of the lowest grades and the least curvature that the country would admit.

The location party in our work on the Union Pacific was followed by the construction corps, grading generally 100 miles at a time. That distance was graded in about 30 days on the plains, as a rule, but in the mountains we sometimes

had to open our grading several hundred miles ahead of our track in order to complete the grading by the time the track should reach it. All the supplies for this work had to be hauled from the end of the track, and the wagon transportation was enormous. At one time we were using at least 10,000 animals, and most of the time from 8000 to 10,000 laborers. The bridge gangs always worked from five to 20 miles ahead of the track, and it was seldom that the track waited for a bridge. To supply one mile of track with material and supplies required about 40 cars, as on the plains everything—rails, tie, bridging, fastening, all railway suppplies, fuel for locomotives and trains, and supplies for men and animals on the entire work—had to be transported from the Missouri River.

Therefore, as we moved westward, every hundred miles added vastly to our transportation. Yet the work was so systematically planned and executed that I do not remember an instance in all the construction of the line of the work being delayed a single week for want of material. Each winter we planned the work for the next season. By the opening of spring, about April 1, every part of the machinery was in working order, and in no year did we fail to accomplish our work. After 1866, the reports show what we started out to do each year, and what we accomplished.

The following extract from a letter written to me by Gen WT Sherman as to what we promised to do in 1867, which was only about one-half what we were prepared to do and did accomplish in 1868, indicates how one year's experience helped us in the progress of the next. It also shows—what the country now seems in a great measure to have forgotten— that the Pacific Railroad, now regarded chiefly in the light of a transcontinental, commercial highway, was then looked upon as a military necessity and as the one thing positively

Below: **This exhibition train is a recreation of the first UP passenger train to run west from the Missouri River.** *At right:* **The steamboats Denver and Colorado unload construction materials for the Union Pacific on the banks of the Missouri River.**

essential to the binding together of the republic East and West:

St Louis, 16 January 1867

My Dear Dodge: I have just read with intense interest your letter of the 14th, and, though you wanted it kept to myself, I believe you will sanction my sending it to General Grant for his individual perusal, to be returned to me. It is almost a miracle to grasp your purpose to finish to Fort Sanders (288 miles) this year, but you have done so much that I mistrust my own judgment and accept yours. I regard this road of yours as the solution of the Indian affairs and the Mormon question, and therefore, give you all the aid I possibly can, but the demand for soldiers everywhere and the slowness of enlistment, especially among the Blacks, limit our ability to respond. Each officer exaggerates his own troubles and appeals for men. I now have General Terry on the upper Missouri, Genral Augur with you, and General Hancock just below, all enterprising young men, fit for counsel or for the field. I will endeavor to arrange so that hereafter all shall act on common principles and with a common purpose, and the first step, of course, is to arrange for the accumulation of the necessary men and materials at the right points, for which your railroad is the very thing. So far as interest in your section is concerned, you may rest easy that both Grant and I feel deeply concerned in the safety of your great national enterprise.

WT Sherman, MG

It was not until after November of 1867, when we had been at work two years, that we got railroad communication with the East at Council Bluffs, Iowa, the initial point of the Union Pacific Railway, by the completion of the Northwestern Railway. Till then, the Missouri River had been the sole route over which supplies could be had. It was available only about three months of the year, and our construction was limited by the quantities of rail and equipment that could be brought to us by boat in that time. In twelve months of work after we had rail communication, we located, built and equipped 587 miles of road, working only from one end, transporting everything connected with it an average distance of 800 miles west of the Missouri River. This feat has not yet been surpassed. In accomplishing it we crossed the divide of the continent and two ranges of mountains, one of which was the Wasatch, where in the winter of 1868-69 we had to blast the earth the same as the rocks.

Indian Troubles

Our Indian troubles commenced in 1864 and lasted until the tracks joined at Promontory. We lost most of our men and stock while building from Fort Kearney to Bitter Creek. At that time every mile of road had to be surveyed, graded, tied and bridged under military protection. The order to every surveying corps, grading, bridging and tie outfit was never to run when attacked. All were required to be armed, and I do not know that the order was disobeyed in a single instance, nor did I ever hear that the Indians had driven a

THE
UNION PACIFIC RAILROAD COMPANY
Proclaims to
FARMERS
Who have spent years grubbing stumps or picking stones, or who pay annually as much rent as will purchase a farm in Nebraska; to
Mechanics
Who find it hard work to make both ends meet at the end of a year's toil, and to EVERYBODY wishing a comfortable home in a healthy, fertile State:
NEBRASKA!
Is destined to be one of the leading Agricultural States in the Union, and greatest beyond the Mississippi; Because,

1st. The land does not have to be cleared of stumps and stones, but is ready for the plow, and yields a crop the first year.
2d. The soil is a deep loam of inexhaustible fertility.
3d. Water is abundant, clear and pure.
4th. The productions are those common to the Eastern and Middle States.
5th. Fruits, both wild and cultivated, do remarkably well.
6th. Stock Raising is extensively carried on and is very profitable.
7th. Market facilities are the best in the West. The great mining regions of Wyoming, Colorado, Utah and Nevada are supplied by farmers of Nebraska.
8th. Coal of excellent quality is found in vast quantities on the line of the road in Wyoming, and is furnished to settlers at cheap rates.
9th. Timber is found on all streams and grows rapidly.
10th. No fencing is required by law.
11th. The climate is mild and healthful; malarial diseases are unknown.
12th. Education is Free.

TICKETS By way of Columbus and Chicago and St. Louis will be furnished at reduced rates for persons desiring to prospect and select lands in Nebraska.

To those who purchase 160 Acres of the Company on Cash or Five Years' Terms, a rebate not to exceed Twenty Dollars, will be allowed on price paid for Ticket.

FREIGHT: Reduced Rates given on Household Goods, Live Stock, Farming Tools, Trees and Shrubbery, in Car Loads, for Settlers' use.

LEAVITT BURNHAM, Land Commissioner U. P. R. R.

The Union Pacific Railroad and Branches.

Best Equipped, Most Direct and Popular Route to the Rich Mineral Districts, Grazing and Farming Regions and to the Famous Pleasure Resorts and Hunting Grounds of the Rocky Mountain Country.

THE COLORADO CITIES AND RESORTS are best reached via the UNION PACIFIC RAILROAD, Colorado Division. By far the most direct, pleasant and popular route to Ft. Collins, Estes Park, Boulder, Golden, Denver, Central, Georgetown, Idaho Springs and Leadville. Best Hunting, Fishing and Pleasure Resorts in sight of the Union Pacific.
THE BLACK HILLS.—The Sidney Stage Line, in connection with the Union Pacific Railroad, affords the shortest, quickest, and the only safe and pleasant stage journey to Rapid City, Custer, Rochford, Deadwood, Crook City, and other prominent points in the Hills, being the only line passing along the entire length of the Hills.
UTAH, IDAHO AND MONTANA.—The UNION PACIFIC, connecting with the UTAH CENTRAL at Ogden, for Salt Lake City, Frisco, Leeds, and all points in Utah, and with the UTAH & NORTHERN, for the Snake and Salmon River Mines, as well as Helena, Deer Lodge, Virginia, Butte City, Glendale, Bozeman, and all the best mining and Agricultural regions in Montana.
CALIFORNIA, ARIZONA, OREGON AND WASHINGTON.—The UNION and CENTRAL PACIFIC RAILROADS form the only line across the continent, to all points in Nevada, California, Oregon, Washington; and in connection with the Southern Pacific, affords a through rail route to the heart of Arizona; or in connection with the finest Steamship lines, to China, Japan and India.

For information concerning the Resources, Climate, and other attractions of the Great West, address THOS. L. KIMBALL, General Passenger and Ticket Agent U. P. R. R., Omaha, Neb.

Reproduced full page advertisement (printed in 1879) appearing in booklet

The Commerce of Two Cities, the Present and Future of Council Bluffs and Omaha

FARMS AND HOMES
IN KANSAS!
EMIGRANTS, LOOK TO YOUR INTERESTS.
FARMS AT $3 PER ACRE,
AND NOT A FOOT OF WASTE LAND!
Farms on Ten Years Credit!
And on Purchase, no portion of the Principal Required.

Lands not Taxable for Six Years!!

FARMING LANDS IN
EASTERN KANSAS,
But one hour's ride from the city of Atchison and the Missouri river, are offered on terms which guarantee to the Actual Settler larger benefits than can be secured under the Homestead Act.

THE CENTRAL BRANCH UNION PACIFIC R. R. CO.,
Offer for Sale their Lands in the Celebrated
KICKAPOO INDIAN RESERVATION,
Situated in the counties of Atchison, Brown and Jackson, in the State of Kansas, on the line of the Central Branch Union Pacific R. R. This tract is 22 miles in length and 12½ miles in width, and contains

152,417 ACRES.

This tract of land is situated just twenty miles west of Atchison, and is distant from Leavenworth and St. Joseph but thirty-five miles. It is intersected by all the old lines of communication between the east and the far west, to-wit: The Great Military Road from Ft. Leavenworth to Ft. Kearney, the Overland Mail Route to California and Colorado, the Emigrant road from St. Joseph, and now the C. B. U. P. R. R. passes through the tract in a northwest course, on the line of which, within its limits, arrangements have been made for the building up of three enterprising towns. At MUSCOTAH and NETAWAKA neat and commodious depot buildings have been erected, and other substantial improvements are in progress. The establishing of

Schools and Churches
At convenient points on the Company's lands will be encouraged and generously assisted. It is stipulated in the treaty with the Kickapoo tribe of Indians, by which the Railroad Co. acquire title to these lands, that they shall be and remain

FREE FROM TAXATION FOR SIX YEARS!
or until patents are issued by the U. S. Government. These peculiar advantages are applicable to and can only be obtained by settlers on the Kickapoo Indian Reservation, who, in addition, have all the advantages which are offered to settlers upon lands in any other locality in Kansas and the west. The Walnut, Grasshopper, Wolf and Nemaha rivers have their source in the northern portion of this body of land. The two former traverse its entire length in a Southeasterly course, and flow into the Kansas river. The two latter flow Northwest into the Missouri river. These several water courses and their tributaries within the limits of this tract of land are upwards of 200 miles in length, the banks of which are skirted with a variety of timber, principally of Oak, Walnut, Hickory, Maple, Hackberry and Elm, making this the

BEST WATERED AND TIMBERED TRACT OF LAND IN NORTHERN KANSAS.
The soil is of Inexhaustible Depth and Unsurpassed Fertility, and the advantages which these lands offer for

AGRICULTURAL AND STOCK RAISING PURPOSES,
are unsurpassed. The country surrounding this tract of land has been settled for many years, and numerous Towns and Villages have grown up on its border, the largest of which is the enterprising town of Hiawatha, Brown county. The other places are Grenada, Kennekuk, Claytonville and Eureka. The fact that the C. B. U. P. R. R. is the best constructed road west of the Mississippi river, is in part attributable to the character of the masonry, the material for which was obtained from the numerous FINE QUARRIES OF STONE which have been opened on the Company's lands. The presence of COAL in various localities on the land gives promise of an abundant supply for domestic and mechanical purposes. The attention of those arranging for emigration to the West

AND SETTLEMENT IN COLONIES
Is especially invited to the advantages which are here offered. The subscriber is authorized to offer

EXTRAORDINARY INDUCEMENTS
To persons applying to purchase homes for immediate improvement. To such, FROM FOUR TO TEN YEARS' CREDIT will be given. The land has been appraised mostly from $3 to $15 per acre, average price less than $7 per acre.

EMIGRANTS, STOP AT ATCHISON CITY, KANSAS,
And confer with the subscriber, who will grant you every facility to acquaint yourselves with the superior advantages which the C. B. U. P. R. R. Co. offer to settlers on their lands. Remember that this Kickapoo Reserve tract is but the first installment of upwards of

1,000,000 ACRES OF LAND
On the line of this road, which the Company are preparing to offer for settlement ON TERMS TO SUIT PURCHASERS. For full information, Maps, Circulars, &c., address

W. F. DOWNS,
Atchison, Kansas, May, 1867.   [4]   Land Commissioner, C. B. U. P. R. R. Co.

PLEASE TO CIRCULATE.   Daily Free Press Print, Atchison, Kansas.

party permanently from its work. I remember one occasion when they swooped down on a grading outfit in sight of the temporary fort of the military some five miles away, and right in sight of the end of the track. The government commission to examine that section of the completed road had just arrived, and the commissioners witnessed the fight. The graders had their arms stacked on the cut. The Indians leaped from the ravines, and, springing upon the workmen before they could reach their arms, cut loose the stock and caused a panic. General Frank Blair, General Simpson and Doctor White were the commissioners, and they showed their grit by running to my car for arms to aid in the fight. We did not fail to benefit from this experience, for, on returning to the East the commission dwelt earnestly on the necessity of our being protected.

The operating department also had the Indians to contend with. An illustration of this came to me after our track had passed Plum Creek, 200 miles west of the Missouri River. The Indians had captured a freight train and were in possession of it and its crews. It so happened that I was coming down from the front with my car, which was a traveling arsenal. At Plum Creek station word came of this capture and stopped us. On my train were perhaps 20 men, some a portion of the crew, some who had been discharged and sought passage to the rear. Nearly all were strangers to me. The excitement of the capture and the reports coming by telegraph of the burning of the train brought all men to

Recognizing that it needed thriving commerce along its lines, the UP and its branch lines encouraged skilled emigrants to settle in the West, as evidenced by the two ads above. *Far left:* An American-type 4-4-0 locomotive, the most common locomotive of its day, near Columbus, Nebraska in 1892.

the platform, and when I called upon them to fall in, to go forward and retake the train, every man on the train went into line, and by their demeanor, showed that they were all ex-soldiers. We ran down slowly until we came in sight of the train. I gave the order to deploy as skirmishers, and at the command they went forward as steadily and in as good order as we had seen soldiers climb the face of Kenesaw under fire, and with great effect.

Aid from the Army

From the beginning to the completion of the road, our success depended in a great measure on the cordial and active support of the Army, especially its commander in chief, General Grant, and the commander of the military Division of the West, General Sherman. He took a personal interest in the project. He visited the work several times each year during its continuance, and I was in the habit of communicating with him each month, detailing my progress

and laying before him my plans. In return I received letters from him almost every month.

We also had the cordial support of the district commanders of the country through which we operated–General Augur, General Cook, General Gibbon, and General Stevenson, and their subordinates. General Grant had given full and positive instructions that every support should be given to me, and General Sherman, in detailed instructions, practically left it to my own judgment as to what support should be given by the troops on the plains. They were also instructed to furnish my surveying parties with provisions from the posts whenever our provisions should give out. The subordinate officers, following the example of their chiefs, responded to every demand made, no matter at what time of day or night,

Far left: **General Ulysses S Grant, commander of the Union Army during the Civil War and US President from 1868-76, was a good friend of Grenville Dodge.** *At right:* **The directors of the Union Pacific confer in their private car.** *Below:* **A UP 0-4-0 Pony Locomotive.**

or time of year or weather, and took as much interest in the matter as we did.

General Sherman's great interest in the enterprise originated from the fact that, in 1849, he personally took charge of (from General Smith, commander on the Pacific coast) the instructions to Lieutenants Warner and Williamson of the engineers (who made the first surveys coming east from California) to ascertain, if possible, whether it was practicable to cross the Sierra Nevada range of mountains with a railroad. These instructions were sent at General Sherman's own suggestion, and the orders and examination preceded the act of Congress making appropriations for explorations and surveys for a railroad route from the Mississippi River to the Pacific Ocean by four years. General Sherman's interest lasted during his lifetime, and was signalized in the closing days of his official life by a summary of transcontinental railroad construction, the most exhaustive paper on the subject I have ever seen.

Passage through the Mountains

When I took charge as chief engineer of the Union Pacific Railway in 1866, I knew that my first duty would be to determine the crossing of the line over the Black Hills—a bold, high spur of the Rocky Mountains—and I concentrated my engineering forces for that purpose. It had already been ascertained that we could get down to the Laramie Plains from the summit going west, but the route had not been determined going east. In my examinations made while

Below: A Union Pacific time schedule effective, 1 June 1868, for the run from North Platte, Nebraska to Cheyenne, Wyoming. At right: General William T Sherman, a frequent correspondent of Major General Grenville M Dodge, chief engineer for the Union Pacific.

coming home from the Powder River expedition in 1865, I had found what I believed to be the most practicable route from the summit to the foot of the mountains on the east, and directed that it be examined. This was immediately done, and the route was found practicable.

After the battle of Atlanta, my assignment to the Department of the Missouri brought the country between the Missouri River and California under my command, and then I was charged with the Indian campaigns of 1865 and 1866. I traveled again over all that portion of the country I had explored in former years, and saw the beginning of that great future that awaited it. I then began to comprehend its capabilities and resources; and in all movements of our troops and scouting parties I had reports made upon the country—its resources and topography—and I myself, during the two years, traversed it east and west, north and south—from the Arkansas to the Yellowstone, and from the Missouri to the Salt Lake basin.

It was on one of these trips that I discovered the pass through the Black Hills and gave it the name of Sherman, in honor of my great chief. Its elevation is 8236 feet, and for years it was the highest point reached by any railroad in the United States. The circumstances of this accidental discovery may not be uninteresting.

While returning from the Powder River campaign, I was in the habit of leaving my troops and trains, and with a few men, examining all the approaches and passes from Fort Laramie south, over the secondary range of mountains known as the Black Hills—the most difficult to overcome with proper grades of all the ranges, on account of short slopes and great height. When I reached Lodge Pole Creek (up which went the Overland Trail), I took a few mounted

---

UNION PACIFIC RAILROAD
LODGE POLE DIVISION.
TIME SCHEDULE NO. 12.
TO TAKE EFFECT MONDAY, JUNE 1st, 1868, AT 3:30 O'CLOCK A. M.

For the government and Information of Employes only. The Company reserves the right to vary therefrom at pleasure.

Trains Leave Omaha and Laramie Daily, Sundays Excepted.

BOUND WEST				Dist. from North Platte	NAMES OF STATIONS	Dist. from Cheyenne	BOUND EAST			
NO.7 FREIGHT	NO.5 FREIGHT	NO.3 EXPRESS	NO.1 FREIGHT				NO.2 FREIGHT	NO.4 EXPRESS	NO.6 FREIGHT	NO.8 FREIGHT
5:30 P. M.	1:15 P. M.	7:00 A. M	10:45 P. M.		NORTH PLATTE	225	3:50 A. M.	7:30 P. M.	12:45 P. M.	10:45 P. M.
					16.56					
6:50	2.35	7:45	12:00 M.	16.56	O'FALLONS	208.43	2:45	6:50	11:35 A. M.	9:20
					14.40					
8:00	3:55	8 20	1:50 A. M.	30.97	ALKALI	194.03	1:50	6:15	10:30	8:00
					19.24					
9:40	5:30	9.00	3:20	50.22	OGALALLA	174.78	12:45 A. M.	5:30	9:00	5:30
					19.30					
11:30	6:55	9:45	4:50	69.52	BIG SPRING	155.47	11:30 P. M.	4:40	7:30	4:15
					16.50					
12.40 A. M.	8:05	10:30	6:10	86.03	JULESBURG	138.97	10:30	4.00	6:10	3:15
					19.13					
2 00	9:20	11:15	7:35	105.17	LODGE POLE	119.83	9:20	3:10	4:40	1:50
					17.71					
3:15	10:45	12:00 M.	9.00	122.88	SIDNEY	102.12	8.00	2:25	3:15	12:30
3.35	11 05	12:20 P. M.	9.15	122.88	SIDNEY	102.12	7:45	2:00	2:45	12:20 P. M.
					18.85					
5:15	12:40 A. M.	1:05	10:45	141.73	POTTER	83 26	6.10	1 05	12:40 A. M.	10:45 A. M.
					18.22					
6.45	2:00	1:50	12:15 P. M.	159.95	ANTELOPE	65.04	4:45	12 15 P. M.	10:10 P. M.	9:00
					11 94					
8:00	3:00	2:15	1:15	171.90	BUSHNELL	53 09	3 45	11:45 A. M.	8:50	8:00
					10.00					
9:20	4:00	2:45	2:45	181.90	PINE BLUFF	43.09	2:45	11:15	7:35	6:35
					11.11					
10:45	5:10	3:10	4:00	193.02	EGBERT	31.97	1:30	10:45	6:30	5:10
					12.03					
12:15 P. M.	6:15	3:35	5:20	205 05	HILLSDALE	19.94	12:15 P. M.	10:10	5:20	4:00
					11.54					
1:15	7:15	4:10	6:20	216.60	ARCHER	8.39	11:30 A. M.	9:40	4:10	2:45
					8.39					
2:00	8:00	4:30	7:00	225 00	CHEYENNE		10.50 A. M.	9:15 A. M.	3:30 P. M.	2:00 A. M.

C. H. MUCHMORE, Master Transportation.   H. M. HOXIE, Ass't Sup't.   W. SNYDER, Gen'l Sup't.

men—I think six—and with one of my scouts as guide, went up the creek to the summit of Cheyenne Pass, striking south along the crest of the mountains on what was known as the Saint Vrain and the Laramie Trail.

About noon, in the valley of a tributary of Crow Creek, we discovered Indians, who, at the same time, discovered us. They were between us and our trains. I saw our danger and took means immediately to reach the ridge and try to head them off, and follow it to where the cavalry could see our signals. We dismounted and started down the ridge, holding the Indians at bay, when they came too near, with our Winchesters. It was nearly night when the troops saw our smoke signals of danger and came to our relief; and, in going to the plains without a break, I said to my guide that if we saved our scalps I believed we had found the crossing of the Black Hills—and over this ridge, between Lone Tree and Crow creeks, the wonderful line over the mountains was built. For over two years, all explorations had failed to find a satisfactory crossing of this range. The country east of it was unexplored, but we had no doubt we could reach it.

The year 1866 was spent in determining the crossing of the Rocky Mountains or the Black Hills, and the approaches to them from the east. It was the great desire of the company to build the line through Denver, Colorado if possible, up the South Platte Valley and crossing the mountains west of Denver, and reaching Salt Lake by the Yampa, White and Uinta valleys, and I covered the country from the Laramie Canyon on the north to the Arkansas on the south, examining all the mountain passes and approaches. . .personally.

These surveys demonstrated that there was no question as to where the line should cross these mountains. The general examination of the plains along the east foot of the

mountains showed that the plains rose from the Arkansas northward until they reached their apex at the valley of Crow Creek, near where Cheyenne now stands. Then they fell to the north toward the Laramie, and when we came to examine the summits of these mountains, we found their lowest altitude was in the vicinity of the Cheyenne Pass, so that there was no question as to where our line should run.

The line up the Platte, up the Lodge Pole and by the Lone Tree Pass, which I had discovered, was far superior to any other line, and it forced us to abandon the line in the direction of Denver, and we had in view the building of a branch from Crow Creek to Denver, about 112 miles long.

I reported the result of my examination on 15 November 1866 to the company, and on 23 November 1866 the company adopted the lines which I had recommended, and I immediately proceeded to develop them for building the next year. We also examined. . . the line by way of the North Platte, Fort Laramie, Sweet Water Creek and the South Pass, reaching Salt Lake by the way of the Big Sandy and Black Fork. This line avoided the crossing of the Black Hills and the heavy grade ascending from the east to the summit and the 90-foot grade dropping down into the Laramie plains, but this line was some 40 miles longer than the direct line by the Lodge Pole, and on this line there was no development of coal as there was on the line adopted by the company, and on presenting this question to the government, they decided against the North Platte and South Pass line.

The chiefs of parties for this work were: James A Evans, who was an engineer of great ability; and Mr PT Brown, who was an assistant engineer. This young man had started out in 1864 as a rodman. He made the surveys through Clear Creek to the Middle Park, over the Burthud Pass; also the Boulder Pass. On this pass in November, the party was caught in the severest snow storm known in the mountains, and he was obliged to abandon his pack train and save his party by working his way eastward through the storm to Boulder Creek. His stock drifted to Middle Park. There they wintered near the hot springs. I received knowledge of this through one of my old mountain friends that they were there in good condition, and we recovered them in the spring.

Mr LL Hills, assistant engineer, had charge of the surveys on the Lodge Pole line and up the Cache La Poudre River to Laramie Plains, and Mr JE House had charge of the surveys, soundings, and examination of the Missouri River. Mr FA Case, division engineer, was completing the examination of the passes through the main range, made the year before, and Mr FH Ainsworth was running the lines in the Platte Valley, while Mr Thomas H Dates had charge of the surveys in Utah and west to the California state line. The explorations and surveys of 1866 had only confirmed the reconnaissance, made in the 1850s by Mr Dey and myself, of the general route of the Union Pacific Railroad— so that for the years to come our work would be almost entirely devoted to the final locations.

In the spring of 1867 I received a letter from General Grant, suggesting that in my explorations during the year 1867, I take with me his Chief of Staff, General John A Rawlins, for the benefit of his health. General Rawlins had shown a tendency toward consumption, and it was thought that three or four months in camp on the plains would be of great benefit to him. I therefore with great pleasure invited General Rawlins to accompany me, with such friends as he might select. He came to me at Omaha, bringing with him

Major JW McK Dunn, ADC, and John E Corwith, of Galena, Illinois, and added to this party, on my invitation, was John R Duff, son of a director of the road, and Mr David Van Lennep, my geologist.

We had as an escort two companies of cavalry and two of infantry, under the command of Lieutenant Col JK Mizner, who had with him Lieutenant JW Wheelan and Dr Henry N Terry, Assistant Surgeon, US Army. They accompanied me during the entire summer. We started out on the first of June and went to the end of the track, which was then at North Platte, and from there, we marched immediately up the Platte, then up the Lodge Pole to the east base of the Black Hills, where we were joined by General CC Augur…with his staff. General Augur's instructions were to locate the military post where I located the end of the division, and after a thorough examination of the country at the east base of the mountains, I located the division point on Crow Creek, where Cheyenne now stands, and named it Cheyenne. General Augur immediately located,

just north of the town, the military post of DA Russell. We spent the Fourth of July at this place, and General John A Rawlins delivered a very remarkable and patriotic speech.

Another Skirmish with the Indians

While we were camped here the Indians swooped down out of the ravine of Crow Creek and attacked a Mormon grading train and outfit that was coming from Salt Lake to take work on the road and killed two of its men. Our cavalry hastily mounted and drove off the Indians and saved their stock. We buried the men and started the graveyard of the future city, now the capital of the state of Wyoming.

In the spring of 1867 there was a party in the field under LL Hills running a line east from the base of the Rocky Mountains. The first word I received from it was through the commanding officer at Camp Collins, who had served under me while I commanded the department. He informed me that a young man named JM Eddy had brought the party into that post, its chief having been killed in a fight with the

Indians. I inquired who Eddy was and was informed that he was an axman in the party, and had served under me in the Civil War. I ordered him to meet me with his party on the Lodge Pole as I traveled west. He turned out to be a young boy who had entered the 'Thirteenth Illinois' when only 16 or 17. The fight in which Mr Hills, the chief, was killed occurred some six miles east of Cheyenne, and after the leader was lost young Eddy rallied the party and by the force of his own character took it into Camp Collins. Of course I immediately promoted him. He was with me during the entire construction of the Union Pacific, rising from one position to another, until he became the General Manager of portions of the great Southwestern system. He died in the railroad service.

After meeting this party, I completed the location of the line to Crow Creek, at the foot of the mountains, now known as Cheyenne.

We marched west across the Black Hills and Laramie Plains and passed through Rattle Snake Hills Pass, following

down a stream that emptied into the Platte just opposite Fort Steele, and at a point where the Union Pacific now crosses the North Platte River. We crossed this stream by swimming our horses and proceeded west. The country from the Platte west to the Bitter Creek is very dry, no running water in it, and before we reached camp, General Rawlins became very thirsty, and we started out in an endeavor to find running water, and I discovered a spring in a draw near where the town of Rawlins now stands. When General Rawlins reached this spring he said it was the most gracious and acceptable of anything he had had on the march, and also said that if anything was ever named for him, he wanted it to be a spring of water, and I said then, 'We will name this Rawlins Springs.' It took that name. The end of one of our divisions happened to be close to this spring, and I named the station

Below: **This Union Pacific 4-4-0 Camel Locomotive was built by Rogers of Paterson, New Jersey in 1887. Notice that the engineer's cab sits astride the boiler like a camel's hump, hence the 'Camel' appellation.**

Rawlins, which has grown now into quite a town and a division point of the Union Pacific road.

As soon as I had determined the line over the Black Hills, I learned that one of the parties which was trying to work west from the North Platte had found the maps of the country misleading. Endeavoring to find the summit of the continental divide, this party had dropped into a great basin. Percy T Brown, the chief of the party, finding himself in an unknown country entirely different in character from what had been expected, took eight of his escort and started to explore the region. When near the center of what is now known as the Red Desert, he was attacked by 300 Sioux Indians working south to the Bridger Pass stage road coming from the Sweetwater. Brown took measures to defend himself, occupying, after a severe contest with the Indians for its possession, a small hill, and fighting from 12 o'clock noon until toward night, when he was shot through the abdomen.

He then ordered the soldiers to leave him and save themselves, but they refused, and allowed the Indians to get hold of the stock, after which the redskins withdrew. The soldiers then made a litter of their carbines and packed Brown upon it 15 miles through the sagebrush to Laclere station, near Bridgers Pass. Their laborious efforts to save him were made in vain, however, for Brown died at the station.

Upon an examination of this country, we discovered that the divide of the continent had let down from the Wind River Mountains on the north to Medicine Bow, from the beginning of the main Rocky Mountains on the south from an elevation of 13,000 feet to one of 7000 into an open plain, and that the divide was in reality a great basin about 80 miles across at its widest part east and west, and 100 to 150 miles northwest and southeast at its longest part. The streams running into it sink, leaving a red soil over the entire basin, from which it receives the name of the Red Desert. The Union Pacific Railway crossed the Red Desert near its southern limit, between the stations of Creston and Tipton, a distance of about 34 miles.

Rescue

In the basin we found and rescued the party headed by Thomas F Bates, which was coming from Green River east. When we reached what is now Creston, we discovered Bates and his party. They had been in the widest part of the basin for nearly a week without water, and were almost exhausted. When we discovered them, they had abandoned the line and were taking a course due east by the compass, running for water. At first we thought them Indians, but on looking through my glasses I saw that they had teams with them. We went to their relief at once and saved them. They were in a deplorable condition from thirst.

On the western rim of the basin, as we left it, we ran into the remains of some old wagons and other articles which indicated that some military force had tried to cross there. Afterwards, I learned that it had been Colonel Steptoe's exhibition to Oregon, and that in crossing from Bridgers Pass trying to reach the Northwest, they struck this country and were obliged to abandon a portion of their outfit. This demonstrated that no knowledge of this depression was had by anyone until we developed it in our surveys. We had great

At right: A Union Pacific woodburner briefly pauses by the water tank at the Green River Bridge in Wyoming, in the 1860s. Snow-covered Citadel Rock is prominent in the background.

difficulty in obtaining water for the operation of our road through the basin, being obliged to sink artesian wells to a great depth.

After reaching the west rim of the Red Desert you immediately drop into the valley of Bitter Creek, the waters of which flow into the Pacific. The crossing of the Continental Divide by the Union Pacific is thus by way of an open prairie of comparatively low elevation, about 7000 feet, instead of a mountain range. The work of building the road there was unexpectedly light, and it almost seems that nature made this great opening in the Rocky Mountains expressly for the passage of a transcontinental railroad.

The Push for Completion

The Act of 1862 provided that the Union Pacific and Central Pacific should join their tracks at the California state line. The Act of 1864 allowed the Central Pacific to build 150 miles east of the state line, but that was changed by the Act of 1866, and the two companies were allowed to build, one east and the other west, until they met. The building of 300 miles of road during the summers of 1866 and 1867, hardly 12 months actual work, had aroused great interest in the country and much excitement, in which the government took a part. We were pressed to as speedy a completion of the road as possible, although 10 years had been allowed by Congress.

The officers of the Union Pacific had become imbued with this spirit, and they urged me to plan to build as much road as possible in 1868. I have already alluded to the completion of the Northwestern Railway in December of 1867, to Council Bluffs, Iowa, which gave us an all-rail connection with the East, so that we could obtain our rail material and equipment during the entire year. The reaching of the summit of the first range of the Rocky Mountains (which I named Sherman, in honor of my old commander) in 1867, placed us comparatively near good timber—for ties and bridges—which, after cutting, could be floated down the mountain streams at some points to our crossing, and at others to within 25 or 30 miles of our work. This afforded great relief to the transportation.

In the fall of 1867, when we closed our work and ended our track at the summit of the Black Hills, the company was apparently at their end, so far as finances were concerned, and were greatly disturbed as to the future. When I had received all of my parties' reports, extending to the California state line, and had completed the profiles, maps and estimates, I went on to New York and met the Board of Directors, and when they saw the very favorable line that we had obtained over the Black Hills, across the Laramie Plains and over the divide of the continent, where they had expected to meet very heavy work, and also the line over the Wasatch Range to Salt Lake and from there on west, they were very much encouraged.

The estimates on this line were not more than one-half of what they had expected, and then a few miles west of Cheyenne they would commence receiving $48,000 in government bonds per mile for 150 miles, and from there on $32,000 in government bonds per mile. This was a great advance on the amount that they had received on the 630 miles from the Missouri River to the east base of the mountains (which was only $16,000 in government bonds

The Mormons wanted the UP to pass through Salt Lake City, but Grenville Dodge decided Ogden would be the better route. *At left:* Twentieth century UP 8444, aided by engine 3985, heads to Ogden.

per mile) while the cost of the work had been very heavy, for, on account of the long distance rails, timber, supplies, and everything had to be hauled.

The company immediately made extraordinary effort to provide the money to build to Salt Lake, and during the winter I received instructions to make every effort to build as much line as possible the coming year, and the company forwarded to us at our base on the Missouri River an immense amount of rails, fastenings, etc, as we then had rail connections by the northwestern road all the way to Council Bluffs.

We made our plans to build to Salt Lake, 480 miles, in 1868, and to endeavor to meet the Central Pacific at Humboldt Wells, 219 miles west of Ogden, in the spring of 1869. I had extended our surveys during the years 1867 and 1868 to the California state line, and laid my plans before the company, and the necessary preparations were made to commence work as soon as frost was out of the ground, say about 1 April. Material had been collected in sufficient quantities at the end of the track to prevent any delay. During the winter ties and bridge timber had been cut and prepared in the mountains to bring to the line at convenient points, and the engineering force were started to their positions before cold weather was over, that they might be ready to begin their work as soon as the temperature would permit. I remember that the parties going to Salt Lake crossed the Wasatch Mountains on sledges, and that the snow covered the tops of the telegraph poles. We all knew and appreciated that the task we had laid out would require the greatest energy on the part of all hands.

The Mormons

We had only one controversy with the Mormons, who had been our friends and had given the full support of the church from the time of our first reconnaissances until the final completion. It was our desire and the demand of the Mormons that we should build through Salt Lake City, and we bent all our energies to find a feasible line passing through that city and around the south end of Great Salt Lake and across the desert to Humboldt Wells, a controlling point in the line. In a letter which I received from Mr James R Maxwell, assistant engineer, he makes the following statement of the result of their survey in 1867:

'The boat we used in sounding the lake was made of inch boards and not calked very well, and the heavy water soon shook the calking out of the bottom, and it did seem for a short time that we would have to take to the water. That was on our way back from Promontory Point to Mud Island. After we landed the topographer told me that he could not swim; if I had known that he would not have been on the boat. When I found 22 feet of water where Captain Stansbury had only 10 I knew that that line was not feasible then. I was told by a Mormon Bishop that on two occasions the annual rise was six feet above any previous record and that it remained so, covering thousands of acres of farming land at the northeastern side of the lake.'

This part of the lake that was sounded by this party was east of Promontory Point. The water to the west of Promontory Point being twice as deep as that toward the east, therefore it was impossible for us with our means to build a railroad across the lake and we were forced around the north end of the lake and over Promontory Point....We

had to adopt that route with a view of building a branch to Salt Lake City, but Brigham Young would not have this, and appealed over my head to the Board of Directors, who referred the question to the government directors, who fully sustained me. Then Brigham Young gave his allegiance and aid to the Central Pacific, hoping to bring them around the south end of the lake and force us to connect with them there. He even went so far as to deliver in the Mormon Tabernacle a great sermon denouncing me, and stating that a road could not be built or run without the aid of the Mormons.

When the Central Pacific engineers made their survey they, too, were forced to adopt a line north of the lake. Then President Young returned to his first love, the Union Pacific, and turned all his forces and aid to the road.

Changes in the Route

About 1 April, I went onto the plains myself and started our construction forces, remaining the whole summer between Laramie and the Humboldt Mountains....During the building of the road from Sherman Pass westward, many questions arose in relation to the location, construction, the grades and curvatures of the work. All through, I stood firmly for my line, for what I considered was a commercially economical line for the company, and for what I thought we ought to build under the specifications of the government. News of the contest between the company and the contractors reached Washington through the government commissioners. Generals Grant and Sherman were much interested, and in 1868 they came west with a party consisting of Major General Phillip H Sheridan, General William S Harney, General Louis C Hunt, General Adam Slemmer, Sidney Dillon, and TC Durant, who wired me to meet them at Fort Sanders, then the headquarters of General Gibbon. The questions in dispute between myself and the contractors were then taken up. Generals Grant and Sherman took decided grounds in the matter, supporting me fully, so that I had no further trouble. Probably no more noted military gathering has occurred since the civil war.

Two changes were made by the contractors in the line so as to cheapen the work, and this was at the expense of the commercial value of the property. This was always opposed by the division engineer who located the line, and he was

Below: **The paymaster's car at Promontory, Utah. One in four workers was a track-layer; the others were graders, teamsters, herdsmen, cooks, bakers, blacksmiths, bridge builders, carpenters, masons and clerks.**

supported by the chief engineer. The changes were always made when the chief engineer was absent. The company would agree to a change, and the work on the changes would be so far advanced that it was too late to rectify the matter when the chief engineer returned. The first change was of Mr James A Evans' location on the eastern slope of the Black Hills from Cheyenne to Sherman. Evans had a 90-foot equated grade with a six degree maximum curvature. It was a very fine location, and the amount of curvature was remarkably small for a mountain line. It rose 90 feet to the mile in a steady climb.

Colonel Silas Seymour, the consulting engineer, undertook to reduce this grade to 80 feet, but increased the curvature so much that an engine would haul more cars over Evan's 90-foot grade than on Seymour's 80-foot grade, but Seymour was obliged, when he reached the foot of the mountains, to put in a 90-foot grade to save work as he dropped off the foothills to the plains, and a portion of this grade remains today. When Evans took up the change in his report and compared it with his line, he made it so plain that the change was wrong that the government directors adopted it for their report.

The next change was from the Laramie River to Rattlesnake Hills, or Carbon Summit. The original line ran north of Cooper Lake, and Mr O'Neil, who had instructions to locate on that line, changed it, by order of Colonel Silas Seymour, consulting engineer, to a line dropping into the valleys of Rock Creek and Medicine Bow River, to save work. This increased the length of the line 20 miles and caused the report that we were making the road crooked to gain mileage and secure $48,000 per mile of the bonded subsidy. The amount of grading on this line was about one-half of that on the original line. (During 1903 and 1904, in bringing the Union Pacific line down to a maximum grade of 47 feet to the mile, except over the Wasatch Range and Black Hills, the company abandoned this principal change made by the consulting engineer, and built on or near my original location, saving about 20 miles in distance.)

It was this change that brought Generals Grant and Sherman to see me and insist on my remaining as chief engineer. At the time this change was made, the chief engineer was in Salt Lake, and did not know of it until it was practically graded. He entered his protest and notified the company that he would not submit to such changes without being consulted.

(Editor's Note: The changes here discussed figured in the Credit Mobilier Scandal, which itself is discussed in a later chapter of this text.)

Tracks For The Union Pacific

The track laying on the Union Pacific was a science. Mr WA Bell, in an article on the Pacific Railroads, describes it, after witnessing it, as follows:

'We, pundits of the far east, stood upon that embankment, only about a thousand miles this side of sunset, and backed westward before that hurrying corps of sturdy operators with a mingled feeling of amusement, curiosity and profound respect. On they came. A light car, drawn by a single horse, gallops up to the front with is load of rails. Two men seize the end of a rail and start forward, the rest of the gang taking hold by twos, until it is clear of the car. They come forward

at a run. At the word of command, the rail is dropped in its place, right side up with care, while the same process goes on at the other side of the car. Less than 30 seconds to a rail for each gang, and so four rails go down to the minute. Quick work, you say, but the fellows on the Union Pacific are tremendously in earnest. The moment the car is empty, it is tipped over on the side of the track to let the next loaded car pass it, and then it is tipped back again; and it is a sight to see it go flying back for another load, propelled by a horse at full gallop at the end of 60 or 80 feet of rope, ridden by a young Jehu, who drives furiously.

Close behind the first gang come the gaugers, spikers and bolters, and a lively time they make of it. It is a grand 'anvil chorus' that those sturdy sledges are playing across the plains. It is in a triple time, three strokes to the spike. There are 10 spikes to a rail, 400 rails to a mile, 1800 miles to San Francisco—21 million times are those sledges to be swung; 21 million times are they to come down with their sharp punctuation before the great work of modern America is complete.'

I remember that the progress of the work was then such that Generals Grant and Sherman were very enthusiastic over the belief that we would soon reach the summit of the Wasatch Mountains, but I could not convince them that a junction of the two roads was in sight within a year. When

While the UP Camel locomotive pictured on pages 38-39 was one of the Union Pacific's prime movers of the nineteenth century, this UP Big Boy (below) represented state-of-the-art steam in the twentieth century.

UP 4004

UNION PACIFIC

you consider that not a mile of this division of the road had been located on 1 April 1868; that not a mile of this work had been opened; that we covered in that year over 700 miles of road and built 555 and laid 589 miles of track, bringing all of our material from the Missouri River, it is no wonder that Generals Grant and Sherman could not understand how the problem before us would be so speedily solved.

As each 100 miles of road was completed, there came a general acclaim from all parts of the country to our great encouragement, while from our chiefs in New York there was a continual pressure for speed, they giving us unlimited means and allowing us to stretch our forces out hundreds of miles, no matter what additional cost it made to each mile of road. Then we had the sympathy of the whole Mormon Church with us, Brigham Young giving the matter personal attention, and seeing that the line over the Wasatch Mountains down the canyon and westward was covered by Mormons, to whom we let contracts, and we had the additional incentive that the Central Pacific was coming east nearly as fast as we were going west.

The entire track and a large part of the grading on the Union Pacific Railway was done by the Casement Brothers— General Jack Casement and Dan Casement. General Casement had been a prominent brigade and division commander in the western Army. Their force consisted of 100 teams and 1000 men, living at the end of the track in boarding cars and tents, and moved forward with it every few days.

It was the best organized, best equipped, and best disciplined track force I have ever seen. I think every chief of the different units of the force had been an officer of the Army, and entered on this work the moment they were mustered out. They could lay from one to three miles of track per day,

Below: **This Charles Russell pen and ink sketch depicts a group of mounted Indians eyeing a construction train, circa 1869. The Union Pacific construction crews often had to battle Indian raiders.**

as they had material, and one day laid eight and one-half miles. Their rapidity in track laying, as far as I know, has never been excelled....

They not only had to lay and surface the track, but had to bring forward from each base all the material and supplies for the track, and for all workmen in advance of the track. Bases were organized for the delivery of material generally from 100 to 200 miles apart, according to the facilities for operation. These bases were as follows: first, Fremont; second, Fort Kearney; third, North Platte; fourth, Julesburg; fifth, Sidney; sixth, Cheyenne; seventh, Laramie; eighth, Benton (the last crossing of the North Platte); ninth, Green River; tenth, Evanston; eleventh, Ogden; and, finally, Promontory.

At these bases large towns were established, which moved forward with the bases, and many miles of sidings were put in for switching purposes, unloading tracks, etc. At these prominent points I have seen as many as a thousand teams waiting for their loads to haul forward to the front for the railway force, the government, and for the limited population then living in that country. I have seen these terminal towns seem to rise in population as we went, until, at Cheyenne, where we wintered in 1867-68, there were 10,000 people. From that point they decreased, until, at Green River there were not over 1,000. After we crossed the first range of mountains we moved our bases so rapidly they could not afford to move with us.

One of the most difficult problems we had to solve was to keep sufficient material at the terminals to supply the daily demand. This work fell to Webster Snyder and his assistant, HM Hoxie, who had charge of the operation of the completed road. They were both young men in the business then, but have been at the head of great corporations since. They performed their work successfully and with ability. Hoxie said to me once, in answer to a question: 'We do not take our hand off the throttle night or day until we know the front is supplied.'

Life in the Construction Camp

The construction crews for the Union Pacific came from all sections of the country, as well as from overseas. Crews were composed of Native Americans, German and English immigrants and, following the Civil War, a contingency of newly freed Blacks. But the largest work force was the Irish.

The Irish had been coming to the United States since Colonial times, but the greatest number had fled Ireland during the potato famine of the 1850s. The Irish had worked on the Erie Canal, on the first railroads that crisscrossed the East Coast, and had even fought for both the North and the South during the Civil War. In short, the Irish were to the industrial North what the slaves had been to the agrarian South—labor. When construction for the UP began its westward path, the Irish were there.

The construction camp was in itself a small bustling community. Four huge house cars—eighty-five feet long by by eight feet high and ten wide—formed the heart of the camp. One car was divided into a kitchen, an office, and a dining room. Another was a dining hall with tables and benches running the entire length. A third car was half dining car, half bunk. The fourth car was entirely composed of bunks, three high on both sides of the car, and complete with US Army rifles in the middle.

The crew started their day at sunrise, with a breakfast of beef, beans, potatoes, fresh bread, and gallons of strong coffee or tea. Work began immediately following this hearty fare. Each worker had a specific task to complete. The seasoned hands knew their appointed tasks and the new men were expected to know theirs almost from the start. The crews laid a mile of track a day, with every mile requiring forty carloads of food, tools, and iron. Every morning the trains arrived from Omaha carrying spikes, ties, rails, and chairs. The first iron car pulled in behind the headquarters cars and was immediately unloaded, the material thrown off onto the right of way alongside the track, and thus would begin the assembly line process of unloading, loading and building.

The men were allowed an hour's break for lunch, which consisted of the same fare as breakfast. After a quick smoke or nap, it was back to work until the sun set. Evenings were their own time.

The graders' camps, which were located about a hundred miles beyond the track-layers camps, employed more men. Their daily routine was similar to the track-layers, although accommodations were rougher. There were no bunk cars; workers instead pitched their tents closely together for convenience, as well as protection against Indians. If the camp was large, a semipermanent structure was erected to serve as a kitchen or office.

The grader's task was simple, albeit monotonous: turning up the earth and leveling it for the track-layers behind them. The ground of the prairies proved easy to turn, yielding readily to tools and brawn. Little cutting was needed and rarely were there stream beds requiring heavy filling. Although the task itself was easy to complete, it was made difficult by its repetition. Hour

Above: **Track-laying along the transcontinental route. Union Pacific track-layers laid a mile of track a day and were paid approximately $3 a day for their efforts.**

after hour, the workers toiled over the earth. Like the track-layers, the graders worked from sunrise to sunset, with an hour's break at noon.

The work was brutal by today's standards, but the railroad workers were no worse off than the factory workers in the East, who worked hours just as long and often as dangerous. The UP crews were young and tough, almost all of them having served in the Army and therefore accustomed to the hardships of outdoor living. The food may have lacked variety, but it was plentiful and steady. Above all, the pay was good—up to $2.50 per day. All in all, the worker's life was hard, repetitious and dull. After working from dawn to dusk for six days, he was granted a day of rest on Sunday, but there was not much to do on the plains. A man could spend his free time doing personal chores such as washing or mending, or if he could read and write, he could communicate with friends and families back East. Fun took the form of an occasional buffalo hunt, fishing or swimming in the Platte River, card games and dice. Because so many of the crew were veterans of the Civil War, from both the North and the South, the battles of the war were often refought in the construction camps of the Union Pacific. And of course there was whiskey. The whiskey peddlers did not waste any time in locating the camps and soon most camps were equipped with a primitive saloon, usually a plank stretched across a pair of kegs.

Like General Sherman's Army on its march to the sea, the Union Pacific crew crossed the continent— rough, tough and unstoppable.

Meeting at Promontory and After

I was surprised at the rapidity with which the work was carried forward. Winter caught us in the Wasatch Mountains, but we kept on grading our road and laying our track in the snow and ice at a tremendous cost. I estimated for the company that the extra cost of thus forcing the work during that summer and winter was over $10,000,000, but the instructions I received were to go on, no matter what the cost. Spring found us with the track at Ogden, and by 1 May we had reached Promontory, 534 miles west of our starting point 12 months before. Work on our line was opened to Humbolt Wells, making, in the year, a grading of 754 miles of line.

The Central Pacific had made wonderful progress coming east, and we abandoned the work from Promontory to Humboldt Wells, bending all our efforts to meet them at Promontory. Between Ogden and Promontory, each company graded a line, running side by side, and in some places one line was right above the other. The laborers upon the Central Pacific were Chinamen, while ours were Irishmen, and there was much ill-feeling between them. Our Irishmen were in the habit of firing their blasts in the cuts without giving warning to the Chinamen on the Central Pacific working right above them. From this cause several Chinamen were severely hurt.

Complaint was made to me by the Central Pacific people, and I endeavored to have the contractors bring all hostilities to a close, but, for some reason or other, they failed to do so. One day the Chinamen, appreciating the situation, put in what is called a 'grave' on their work, and when the Irishmen right under them were all at work let go their blast and buried several of our men. This brought about a truce at once. From that time the Irish laborers showed due respect for the Chinamen, and there was no further trouble.

The Final Spike

When the two roads approached in May of 1869, we agreed to connect at the summit of Promontory Point, and the day was fixed so that trains could reach us from New York and California. We laid the rails to the junction point a day or two before the final closing. Coming from the East, representing the Union Pacific, were Thomas C Durant, Vice President; and Sidney Dillon (who had taken a prominent part in the construction of the road from the beginning); and John R Duff, Directors, together with the consulting engineer and a carload of friends. From the West the representatives of the Central Pacific were its President, Leland Stanford; Mr Collis P Huntington; Mr Crocker; Mr Hopkins; Mr Colton and other members of that company; Mr Montague, chief engineer; and a detachment of troops from Camp Douglass in Salt Lake City. The two trains pulled up facing each other, each crowded with workmen who sought advantageous positions to witness the ceremonies, and literally covered the cars. The officers and invited guests formed on each side of the track, leaving it open to the south. The telegraph lines had been brought to that point so that, in the final spiking, as each blow was struck, the telegraph recorded it at each connected office from the Atlantic to the Pacific. Prayer was offered, a number of spikes were driven in the two adjoining rails, each one of the

Below: **The Central Pacific Chinese workers were the target of antagonism from the UP's Irish workers.** *At right:* **A plaque at Promontory, Utah commemorating the driving of the golden spike where the Central Pacific and the Union Pacific met on 10 May 1869.**

prominent persons present taking a hand, but very few hitting the spikes, to the great amusement of the crowd. When the last spike was placed, light taps were given upon it by several officials, and it was finally driven home by the chief engineer of the Union Pacific Railway. The engineers ran up their locomotives until they touched, the engineer upon each engine breaking a bottle of champagne upon the other one, and thus the two roads were wedded into one great trunk line from the Atlantic to the Pacific. Spikes of silver and gold were brought especially for the occasion, and later miniature spikes were manufactured as mementos of the occasion. It was a bright but cold day. After a few speeches, we all took refuge in the Central Pacific cars, where wine flowed freely, and many speeches were made.

Telegrams were sent to President Grant, Vice President Colfax, and other officials throughout the country. I did not fail to send a message to my old commander, who had been such a helpful factor in the building of the road, and I received this message in response:

Washington, May 11, 1869

Gen GM Dodge: In common with millions, I sat yesterday and heard the mystic taps of the telegraph battery announce the nailing of the last spike in the great Pacific road. Indeed, am I its friend? Yea. Yet, am I to be a part of it?—for as early as 1854 I was vice president of the effort begun in San Francisco under contract of Robinson, Seymour & Co. As soon as General Thomas makes certain preliminary inspection in his new command on the Pacific, I will go out, and, I need not say, will have different facilities from that of 1846, when the only way to California was by sail around Cape Horn, taking our ships 196 days. All honor to you, to Durant, to Jack and Dan Casement, to Reed, and the thousands of brave fellows who have wrought out this glorious problem, in spite of changes, storms, and even the doubts of the incredulous, and all the obstacles you have now happily surmounted.

WT Sherman, General

That night the visitors started east and west, leaving the engineers and working parties to arrange the details for conducting the business of each road at this terminal. It was only a day or two before trains bound for the Atlantic and Pacific were passing regularly.

At right: **A crowd gathers around Union Pacific's Number 119 as it prepares to meet Central Pacific's *Jupiter* at Promontory.** *Below:* **East meets West on 10 May 1869. UP's Number 119 appears in the foreground.**

The First Winter

The operation of the road the first winter, 1869-70, gave us a test of what we might expect from the snow. In building the road, we studied the mountains to get our lines upon the slopes that were the least exposed to heavy snows and slides, but we had no means of fighting the snows in the Laramie Plains except by fences and sheds, and none were put up until the year 1870, so that when the heavy snows fell in the winter of 1869-70, six of our trains west of Laramie were snowed in there some weeks.

As a precaution in starting our trains from Omaha, we put on a boxcar with a stove in it and loaded with provisions, so as to meet any emergency. These six trains that were caught in the snow between Laramie and the divide of the continent had these supplies and also were supplied with sledges and snowshoes from Laramie. They had with them, in charge of the six trains, Mr HM Hoxie, the assistant superintendent, who managed to get the trains together, but the blizzards were so many and so fierce that it was impossible for men to work out in the open, and even when they cleared the cuts ahead, they would fill up before they could get the trains through them.

Probably that winter's experience with snow was the worst the Union Pacific has ever experienced, but Mr Hoxie handled his forces with great ability and fed and kept his passengers in good shape. In one train was an opera company bound for California that Mr Hoxie used to entertain the passengers with, so that when the trains reached Salt Lake City, the passengers held a meeting and passed resolutions complimentary to Mr Hoxie and the Union Pacific in bringing them safely through.

The first surveys of the Union Pacific Railway were made in the fall of 1853. The first grading was done in the fall of 1864. The first rail was laid in July of 1865. Two hundred and sixty miles were built in 1866, 240 in 1867, including the ascent of the first range of mountains (to an elevation of 8235 feet above sea level), and from 1 April 1868, to 10 May 1869, 555 miles of road was built, all exclusive of temporary track and sidings, of which over 180 miles was built in addition, all at an approximate cost in cash of about $54 million.

Nearly all the engineers and chiefs of the different units of the construction of the line have risen to distinction in their profession since the road was built. The chiefs of the parties were SB Reed, FM Case, James A Evans, Percy T Brown, LL Hills (the two latter killed by the Indians), JE House, MF Hurd, Thomas H Bates, FC Hodges, James R Maxwell, John O'Neil, Francis E Appleton, Col JO Hudnut, JF McCabe, Mr Morris and Jacob Blickensderfer.

Our principal geologist was David Van Lennep, whose reports upon the geology of the country from the Missouri River to the Pacific have been remarkably verified in later and more detailed examinations.

The superintendents of construction were SB Reed and James A Evans, both of whom had been connected with the road since 1864. They had independent and thorough organizations. Mr SB Reed was a very competent engineer and had had large experience in his profession. He was very successful in utilizing the Mormons in his work west of the Green River. Mr Reed and Mr Hurd afterwards made some of the most difficult locations over the mountain ranges for the Canadian Pacific.

Mr Reed's principal assistant was MF Hurd, who served in the Second Iowa Infantry during the Civil War. I detailed

Above: **The first Union Pacific bridge across the Missouri River between Council Bluffs and Omaha. It had 11 spans—measuring 250 feet each from center to center—and a total length of 2750 feet.**

him on my staff as an engineer, and, although a private, he won distinction in all the campaigns for his ability, nerve, bravery and modesty. On the Union Pacific, as well as other transcontinental lines with which he has been connected, he has performed some remarkable engineering work. He has had to fight many times for the lives of himself and party, and, no matter what odds have been against him, he has never failed to maintain his position and win his battles, though at times the chances looked desperate.

Bridging The Missouri River

During the building of the road, the question of bridging the Missouri River was under discussion, and continuous examinations of the river by sounding, watching currents, etc were undertaken. Three points were finally determined upon as most feasible...Childs Mill, which had a high bridge, was the shortest and reached Muddy Creek with a 35-foot grade, avoiding the heavy 66-foot grade at Omaha...Telegraph Pole, right where there was some rock bottom—this to be a low drawbridge...and the M&M crossing for a high bridge. The latter was decided upon more especially to meet the views of Omaha, and for the aid that

city gave the company.

We began work on the bridge in 1868, and continued it in 1869 and 1870, but the company found it impossible to continue, as they had no funds, and they could not issue any securities under their charter to pay for the work. I was very anxious the bridge should be built to utilize the thousand acres of land I had bought for our terminals in Iowa, and to fix permanently and practically the terminus in Iowa.

The company proposed to me to organize a bridge company to interest the Iowa roads terminating at Council Bluffs, and to ask authority from the government to construct the bridge and issue securities upon it, the Union Pacific agreeing to use the bridge and make its terminals and connections with the Iowa roads on the Iowa side. I incorporated the Council Bluffs Railway and Missouri Bridge Company, and went before Congress for permission to bridge the Missouri River at the M&M crossing. I saw all the Iowa roads. They agreed to give their aid, but made the condition that their connection with the Union Pacific should be on the Iowa side.

I went to Washington, presented the bill, passed it through the House, and left it in Senator Harlan's hands to pass it in the Senate. This was very quietly done, but Omaha got alarmed, and Governor Saunders, who was a personal friend of Senator Harlan, took the matter up, and, I think, went to Washington; the Omaha people interested themselves in stirring up opposition in Council Bluffs. A public meeting was held, at the corner of Broadway and Pearl streets, over which Mr JW Crawford presided. I was very seriously criticized and the independent bridge scheme denounced, the contention being that the bridge should be a part of the Union Pacific, although it was entirely and solely in the interest of Council Bluffs, and would have brought the terminus and business of the Union Pacific to the Bluffs, as they had entered into an agreement with Iowa that reads to that effect.

The public meeting was addressed in favor of the bridge by Messrs Pusey and myself, also Mr Caleb Baldwin and others, and was opposed by Messrs James Montgomery, Larimer and others. The meeting passed resolutions asking our Senators to defeat the bridge bill. Senator Harlan acted on this resolution and defeated the bill in the Senate, and Saunders and Omaha accomplished their work.

The Union Pacific Company was greatly disgusted and disappointed, and dropped for the time all efforts to build a bridge. If the bill had passed the bridge would have been built in the interest of Council Bluffs and the Iowa roads. The Union Pacific later on applied to Congress, which passed a bill authorizing the Union Pacific to build a bridge and to issue bonds and stock upon it—the interest upon them to be paid from the revenue of the bridge—and placed it entirely in their control. The Union Pacific had no great interest in coming to Council Bluffs or Iowa, and made their terminus at Omaha, and forced the Iowa roads over the bridge, until 1875 when the United States Supreme Court decided that the Union Pacific should be operated from Council Bluffs westward as a continuous line for all purposes of communication, travel, and transportation, and especially ordered them to start all through passenger and freight trains westward-bound from the Bluffs.

This came too late to cure the mischief the town meeting had accomplished, as the Union Pacific had its interests centered in Omaha, its offices located there, and the Iowa roads had made their contracts and gone there. The Bluffs have reaped only the benefit of its terminal that the growth of business has granted, whereas by law, by economy of operation and by the ample terminals made to accommodate it, it should have been the actual terminus, and should have received full benefit of it—not only from traffic of the Union Pacific, but from the traffic and interest of the Iowa roads. The Union Pacific completed the first bridge crossing the Missouri River and opened it for traffic on 22 March 1872.

Omaha was selected as the UP's original eastern terminus, and the city has continued to play an important part in the railroad's operations to this day. *At right:* The Union Pacific locomotive shops in Omaha.

The Credit Mobilier Scandal

Thomas Durant and Credit Mobilier: Another View

(Editor's Note: The following is a representation of the issues discussed in this chapter as researched and written by Aaron Klein, a contemporary historian.)

Thomas Durant was named Vice President and General Manager of the newly formed Union Pacific railroad, which was given a charter to build westward from Omaha. Durant then called on his friend George Francis Train to be the UP's public relations man. Train was, if nothing else, an eloquent, persuasive talker. He was also—to put it mildly—rather eccentric, but many who knew him described him as completely mad and a candidate for a straitjacket. In support of the latter view was the fact that he once announced himself a candidate for the office of 'Dictator of the United States.' It was largely through Train's publicizing and glorifying of the Union Pacific that Congress was put in the right mood to amend the Pacific Railroad Act in 1864 to be more generous to the Union Pacific and Central Pacific than the 1862 version had been.

Train supplied Durant and the others in what came to be known as the 'Pacific Railroad Ring' with the idea for the infamous Credit Mobilier. The Credit Mobilier was ostensibly organized as the company contracting for the construction of the railroad. Actually it was a scheme for the inner circle of the Union Pacific to pay themselves for the work done on the railroad. The basic technique was padding estimates. For example, Durant asked Peter Dey, the chief engineer, to prepare estimates for laying track outside of Omaha. Dey first submitted an estimate of $30,000 a mile. Durant then asked Dey to revise the estimates upward to accommodate better specifications. Dey did so until the estimates were up to $60,000 a mile. Then Durant contracted another company to build the track at the $30,000 a mile estimate. The $30,000-per-mile difference was then pocketed by Durant and his cronies. Peter Dey, who had no stomach for this kind of 'boodle,' resigned.

The Credit Mobilier Scandal reached into Congress and as high as the Vice President of the United States. The congressional involvement was largely due to Congressman Oakes Ames of Massachusetts who, with his brother Oliver, supplied shovels to the Union Pacific. Ames invested heavily in Credit Mobilier and gave or sold for a pittance shares of stock to congressmen and such key political figures as Vice President Schulyer Colfax, Speaker of the House James G Blaine (who unsuccessfully ran for President in 1884), two future Vice Presidents (Henry Wilson and Levi P Morton) and one future President (James A Garfield). The first dividend was declared at 100 percent, a figure which no doubt pleased stockholders of every political rank.

In choosing Grenville Dodge to replace Dey, Durant made one of the best decisions of his life. Since Dodge had surveyed the route he knew it well. Under Dodge's direction some real work finally started on the Union Pacific. However, Durant would soon learn that Dodge did things his own way, even against Durant's wishes.

Almost from the beginning, Durant and his 'New York crowd' were in conflict with Ames and his 'Boston crowd.' In 1867, Sidney Dillon, a Boston man, replaced Durant as president of Credit Mobilier, and Oliver Ames became President of Union Pacific. Durant, however, remained as Vice President. Of course, all of this corporate skirmishing did nothing to make Dodge's job any easier, and it almost took the building of the railroad away from him.

Durant, in an attempt to outflank the Boston crowd, persuaded the Union Pacific executive committee to give him authority to assume direct control of the railroad's construction. Armed with this authority, he went out to Cheyenne to take over. Durant probably assumed that since Dodge was in Washington serving in Congress, he could do what he wanted without interference from his chief engineer. One thing Durant had in mind was to lengthen the routes so that he could collect more per-mile subsidy.

Dodge found out what was going on and traveled to Cheyenne on a special train to confront Durant. The two men argued in front of the workers, and Durant endured the humiliation of Dodge announcing in tones loud enough for everyone to hear, 'Durant, you are going to learn that the men working for the Union Pacific will take orders from me and not from you.'

General Ulysses S Grant (who was running for President) was called in to mediate the dispute, and Durant was again humiliated. Durant accused Dodge of wasting the Union Pacific's money. Dodge did not even attempt to answer the charge, replying simply that if anyone changed his lines, he

At right: Samuel B Reed, the Union Pacific's general superintendent of construction, examines the work in progress as the first transcontinental railroad nears completion.

would quit. When Grant, who was certain to be elected President, replied that he wanted Dodge to continue as chief engineer, Durant knew that he had lost.

Durant was on hand for the golden spike ceremomy on 10 May 1869, still in sufficient favor to be one of the ceremonial hammer wielders. Hardly two weeks later, however, he was ousted from the board.

His health deteriorated and he went into semiretirement at his home in the Adirondack Mountains, where he owned a great deal of land. His last scheme, a plan to develop iron and timber in the Adirondacks, included a proposal for a railroad from the Adirondacks into Canada.

Grenville Dodge's Account

The Ames Brothers

In 1865 Oakes and Oliver Ames, of Boston, had become interested in the enterprise, bringing their own fortune and a very large following, and really gave the first impetus to the building of the road. There was no man connected with it who devoted his time and money with the single purpose of benefit to the country and government more than Oakes Ames, and there was never a more unjust, uncalled for, and ungrateful act of Congress than that which censured him for inducing, as it is claimed, members of Congress to take interest in the construction company. It was not necessary

A forgotten monument to forgotten men. The Ames Monument *(below)*, honoring Oakes and Oliver Ames—whose financial support was instrumental in construction of the UP—could no longer be seen by passing trains when trackage was relocated in 1901.

for the company to have influence in Congress, for there was nothing we could ask that Congress did not give anyhow, and it certainly never occurred to him that he might secure benefits from their votes....

The instructions given me by Oliver Ames, the President of the company, were invariably to obtain the best line the country afforded, regardless of the expense. Oakes Ames once wrote me, when it seemed almost impossible to raise money to meet our expenditures: 'Go ahead; the work shall not stop, even if it takes the shovel shop.'

The Ameses were manufacturers of shovels and tools, and their fortunes were invested in that business; and, as we all know, the shovel shop did indeed, 'go.' When the day came that the business of the Ameses should go or the Union Pacific, Oakes Ames said: 'Save the credit of the road; I will fail.'

It took a man of courage and patriotism to make that decision and lay down a reputation and business credit that was invaluable in New England, and one that had come down through almost a century. To him it was worse than death; and it was the blow given by the action of Congress which, followed by others, put him in his grave.

Praise for the Union Pacific

How well our work was performed is shown by the reports of the distinguished commissions appointed by the government to examine the road during its construction and after its completion.

Commissioners Horace Walbridge, SM Felton, CB Comstock, EF Winslow, and JF Boyd examined the road in

1869 to ascertain the sum of money that was necessary to complete the road under the government specifications, and the sum found necessary on the Union Pacific was $1,586,100, and on the Central Pacific $576,650. The amount required on the Union Pacific was only about one-half as much as the chief engineer of that road had found necessary to complete the road under the company's own specifications, and the company not only spent this, but a much larger sum, in the work.

The last commission, composed of Major General GK Warren, US Army; and J Blickensderfer Jr and James Barnes, civil engineers, concluded their report, in part, as follows:

'The foregoing shows that the location of the Union Pacific Railway is in accordance with the law, and…in its different parts is the most direct, central and practicable that would be found from Omaha to the head of Great Salt Lake. Taken as a whole, the Union Pacific Railway has been well constructed. The energy and perseverance with which the work has been urged forward, and the rapidity with which it has been executed, was without parallel, and the country has reason to congratulate itself upon this great work of national importance so rapidly approaching completion under such favorable auspices.'

When the Canadian government determined to build a Pacific railway, they had the Union Pacific examined, and after that examination they provided in their contracts that the Canadian Pacific should be built upon the Union Pacific standards, and when completed should be in its location and construction equal to it, thus paying a high compliment to the builders of the Union Pacific, and after the completion of the Canadian Pacific Railway, engineers of the Union Pacific were selected to examine that road to determine if its construction was up to the standard required.

The Blickensderfer and Clement report made a comparative analysis of the Union Pacific and Central, their location, construction, grade, curvature, etc, giving to the Union Pacific credit for being superior in most of these matters. The last and most critical examination of the location, grades, etc came within the last three years, when, under the reorganized company, it was determined to reduce the grades to a maximum of 47 feet going east or west, except at two points—the 80-foot grade at Cheyenne going west, and the 80-foot grade at the head of Echo Canyon going east.

The President of the Union Pacific, Mr EH Harriman, at a banquet in Denver in 1904, stated that after the three years' examination, and the expenditure of $15 to $20 million to change the grades to a maximum of 47 feet to the mile, it had been demonstrated that not a mile of road had been built to increase the distance and obtain subsidies; and that the location and construction was a credit to the engineers and executive officers who built the road. Mr JB Berry, chief engineer of the Union Pacific Railroad, who had charge of the changes, pays this tribute to the engineers of the road:

'It may appear to those unfamiliar with the character of the country that the great saving in distance and reduction of grade would stand as a criticism of the work of the pioneer engineers who made the original location of the road. Such is not the case. The changes made have been expensive and could be warranted only by the volume of traffic handled at the present day. Too much credit cannot be given General

GM Dodge and his assistants. They studied their task thoroughly and performed it well. Limited by law to a maximum gradient of 116 feet to the mile, not compensated for curvature, they held it down to about 90 feet per mile.

Taking into consideration the existing conditions 35 years ago—lack of maps of the country, hostility of the Indians (which made United States troops necessary for protection of surveying parties) difficult transportation, excessive cost of labor, uncertainty as to probable volume of traffic, limited amount of money and necessity to get the road built as soon as possible—it can be said, with all our present knowledge of the topography of the country, that the line was located with very great skill.'

Of late years there has been a great deal of criticism and comparison of the building of the Union Pacific and Central Pacific railroads, favoring the latter. The theory is that because the Central Pacific had the more challenging Sierra Nevada mountain range to tackle first, it was a more difficult problem financially and physically to handle than the Union Pacific end, but this is a very great mistake.

The Union Pacific had to bring all of its material, ties, bridging, etc from tidewater by rail or by river. They had to build the first 630 miles without any material on its line to aid them except the earth, and for this they received only $16,000 per mile in government bonds. There was no settlement on the line to create any traffic or earnings along the whole distance, which made it very difficult in appealing to the people to buy bonds and furnish money for the company.

In comparison to this, the Central Pacific started at Sacramento with a tidewater base coming right up to it, so that all the material that had to come from foreign or domestic ports had the cheapest rates by sea. Then from Sacramento they had built over the mountains to Virginia City to the great Bonanza mines at Virginia City, which gave them a large traffic at high rates, and gave them very large earnings. Then, again, only a few miles east of Sacramento, the east base of the Sierra Nevada Range commences, and they immediately received $48,000 in government bonds per mile for the 150 miles, and $32,000 in government bonds from there on to Salt Lake, a distance of barely 200 miles more than the 630 miles that the Union Pacific had to build on $16,000 per mile. This favorable condition for the Central Pacific was such that the representatives of that road had very little difficulty in raising all the money they needed and having for nearly one-half of their road a fine traffic to help pay the interest on their bonds.

Grenville Mellen Dodge was one of the legendary American railroading pioneers. A genius engineer, his expertise was crucial not only to the success of the Union Pacific construction effort, but had also proven to be of inestimable value to the railroading strategies of the North in the American Civil War, in which he suffered severe wounds through enemy action. While he did go on to other railroading ventures following his historic service with the UP, Grenville Mellen Dodge had an abiding interest in the affairs and the operations of the railroad he had helped to build to bind the nation together.

Although there is a discrepancy in the historical records of the time, Dodge City, which became one of the most well-known cow towns along the Union Pacific, may well have been named for Major General Grenville Dodge.

Grenville Dodge's Concluding Report—of 1 December 1869—to the United States Government on the Building of the Union Pacific

In 1853 Henry Farnam and TC Durant, the contractors and builders of the Missouri River Railroad in Iowa, instructed Peter A Dey to investigate the question of the proper point for the Mississippi & Missouri River Railroad to strike the Missouri River to obtain a good connection with any route that might be built across the continent. I was assigned to the duty, and surveys were accordingly extended to and up the Platte Valley, to ascertain whether any road built on the central, or then northern, line would, from the formation of the country, follow the Platte and its tributaries over the plains, and thus overcome the Rocky Mountains.

Subsequently, under the patronage of Mr Farnam, I extended the examination westward to the eastern base of the Rocky Mountains and beyond, examining the practicable passes from the Sangre Christo to the South Pass; made maps of the country; and developed it as thoroughly as could be done without making purely instrumental surveys. The practicability of the route, the singular formation of the country between Long's Peak, the Medicine Bow Mountains, and Bridger Pass, on the south, and Laramie Peak and the Sweetwater and Wind river ranges on the north, demonstrated to me that through this region the road must eventually be built. I reported the facts to Mr Farnam, and through his and his friends' efforts, the prospect for a Pacific railroad began to take shape.

In after years, when the war demonstrated the road to be a military necessity, and the government gave its aid in such munificent grants, surveys were extended through the country previously explored, its resources developed, its hidden treasures brought to light, and its capabilities for the building of a railroad to the Pacific fully demonstrated.

In doing this over the country extending from the Missouri River to the California state line, and covering a width of 200 miles, north and south, and on the general direction of the forty-second parallel of latitude, some 15,000 miles of instrumental lines have been run, and over 25,000 miles of reconnaissances made.

In 1863 and 1864 surveys were inaugurated, but in 1866 the country was systematically occupied; and day and night, summer and winter, the explorations were pushed forward through dangers and hardships that very few at this day appreciate, for every mile had to be run within range of the musket, as there was not a moment's security. In making the surveys, numbers of our men, some of them the ablest and most promising, were killed; and during the construction our stock was run off by the hundred, I might say, by the thousand, and as one difficulty after another arose and was overcome, both in the engineering and running and constructing departments, a new era in railroad building was inaugurated.

Each day taught us lessons by which we profited for the next, and our advances and improvements in the art of railroad construction were marked by the progress of the work, 40 miles of track having been laid in 1865,

260 in 1866, 240 in 1867, including the ascent to the summit of the Rocky Mountains, at an elevation of 8235 feet above the ocean; and during 1868, and to 10 May 1869, 555 miles, all exclusive of side and temporary tracks, of which over 180 miles were built in addition.

The first grading was done in the autumn of 1864, and the first rail laid in July of 1865. When you look back to the beginning at the Missouri River, with no railway communication from the East, and 500 miles of the country in advance without timber, fuel, or any material whatever from which to build or maintain a road, except the sand for the bare roadbed itself, with everything to be transported, and that by teams or at best by steamboats, for hundreds and thousands of miles; everything to be created, with labor scarce and high, you can all look back upon the work with satisfaction and ask, 'Under such circumstances could we have done more or better?'

The country is evidently satisfied that you accomplished wonders, and have achieved a work that will be a monument to your energy, your ability, and to your devotion to the enterprise through all its gloomy (as well as its bright) periods, for it is notorious that notwithstanding the aid of the government there

was so little faith in the enterprise that its dark days—when your private fortunes and your all was staked on the success of the project—far exceeded those of sunshine, faith and confidence.

This lack of confidence in the project, even in the West, in those localities where the benefits of its construction were manifest, was excessive, and it will be remembered that laborers even demanded their pay before they would perform their day's work, so little faith had they in the payment of their wages, or in the ability of the company to succeed in their efforts. Probably no enterprise in the world has been so maligned, misrepresented and criticized as this; but now, after the calm judgment of the American people is brought to bear upon it, unprejudiced and unbiased, it is almost without exception pronounced the best new road in the United States.

Its location has been critically examined, and although the route was determined upon in a comparatively short time—as compared with that devoted to other similar projects—yet, in regard to the correctness of the general route, no question is ever raised; and even in the details of its location, 730 miles of which were done in less than six months, it has received the praise of some of the ablest engineers of the country.

Its defects are minor ones, easily remedied, and all the various commissions, some of them composed of able and noted engineers, have given the company due credit in this particular, although they may have attacked it in others, and today, as in the past, the company need fear no fair, impartial criticism upon it or no examination made by men of ability and integrity or such as are masters of their profession. That it yet needs work to finally complete it no one denies, but whatever is necessary has been, or is being, done.

Its future is fraught with great good. It will develop a waste, will bind together the two extremes of the nation as one, will stimulate intercourse and trade and bring harmony, prosperity and wealth to the two coasts. A proper policy, systematically and persistently followed, will bring to the road the trade of the two oceans, and will give it all the business it can accommodate, while the local trade will increase gradually until the mining, grazing, and agricultural regions through which it passes will build up and create a business that will be a lasting and permanent support to the country.

Below: Union Pacific 8444 passenger train crosses the country, as the UP has done for over a 100 years. With UP's completion, the dream to link the country's borders was fulfilled.

The Golden Age of Railroading

The Wild West

The era between the Civil War and World War I was a time of tremendous growth for the railroad industry. It was also a very complex period in the country's history, as the nation underwent the immense transformation from an agrarian society to an industrial one. This was the era of the Wild West, when hundreds of pioneer towns grew up along the lines of the great Union Pacific Railroad.

Because it was largely responsible for the growth of the West, the coming of the Union Pacific also hastened the end of the American Frontier. In 1869, the dream of a transcontinental railroad had finally been realized, but the territory crossed by the UP was isolated, barren and untamed. The West now comes to mind as a heroic drama of crews battling Indians, as well as the forces of nature, against a backdrop of the plains and mountains. Despite this untamed nature of the West, and perhaps for some because of it, pioneers traversed the prairies and plains in increasingly greater numbers.

The land along the UP was generally perceived as ill-suited for farming but ideal for grazing. Cattlemen were persuaded of the advantage of raising their stock near the railroad, and the UP became a vital link in the process of transporting grass-fed beef to the Chicago markets.

The refrigerator car first appeared in 1867, and enabled, within a few years, meat and produce to be shipped to markets across the country. By claiming that the land along the Union Pacific Railroad was the best in the country for cattle raising, the railroad's government directors boosted the growth of the livestock industry—by 1880 over 90,000 cattle, 85,000 sheep and 3000 horses and mules could be found near the Union Pacific road. The same area had a total of 500 head in 1867.

The cattle business triggered the growth and development of numerous western communities between Evanston, Wyoming and North Platte, Nebraska. In 1868 close to a thousand cattle were herded into the area near North Platte, Nebraska, and one of the first 'cow towns' was born. Other cattle ventures soon followed, and by 1870 roughly 7000 head of cattle were grazing on the plains between Plum Creek and Sidney, Nebraska. The cattle boom continued, and communities spread to western Nebraska and eastern Wyomimg. Ogallala, Nebraska, on the main line of the Union Pacific, became known as one of the leading cow towns in the West. To some extent, the cow towns of the Old West lived up to the Easterner's image of rough and dangerous places, complete with cowboys and Indians, shootouts on Main Street and cattle storming through the center of town.

However, the existence of the cow towns along the western railroads was short-lived. Although the land was excellent for grazing and had supported the buffalo for centuries, overgrazing by cattle and sheep utterly defoliated the land, and within 20 years of the railroads' appearance on the prairie, the buffalo, too, was close to extinction (not only from lack of grazing land, but also from the depredations of men who killed them by the herd for bounty fees). The long cattle drives up the Chisholm Trail from Texas through Kansas, to Nebraska along the Union Pacific tracks were outdated by more modern means of transporting the stock. Ironically, the railroad's influence both created and destroyed the industry.

Recognizing that its survival was now dependent on having thriving towns along its lines, the UP established a land department to encourage settlement in the West. In order to populate the territory, land was sold at low prices— an average of $5 an acre—and settlers eagerly came forward to purchase their piece of America. Land sold quickly along the first two hundred miles of the line, and then the UP was faced with the task of selling what was still perceived as the 'Great American Desert.' By 1875, land sales were down, but passenger travel was booming.

Passenger Service Begins

The first UP passenger trains west of the Missouri sported a locomotive, mail and baggage car, passenger coach, sleeper and business car. The trains held 110 passengers for a fare of $63.33 per passenger. Second-class, or 'emigrant,' tickets cost a mere $26.81, but the coaches were hitched to freight trains and the trip took four to six days (depending on the direction) instead of the usual sixty hours by first class. The trip across the entire country, from New York to San Francisco, took just over a week and cost $150. By today's standards the trip would be a nightmare, but compared to earlier excursions across the country, the train ride was a dream come true. A year after the meeting at Promontory, the fare across the country had been reduced

At right: **When the Union Pacific moved west, numerous 'cow towns' sprang up along its lines as the railroad became an integral part of the cattle industry, moving the grass-fed stock to the eastern markets.**

to $136 for first class and $110 for emigrants, who now were afforded the luxury of traveling by passenger trains rather than by freight trains, a change that reduced travel time by half.

Comfort came to the Union Pacific in the form of Pullman's Palace Cars. These luxurious new sleeper cars had plush, ornate interiors and richly painted exteriors. In 1867, George Pullman, along with Andrew Carnegie, approached Durant with the idea of sleeper cars. Union Pacific's response was a contract requiring that the Pullman cars be kept under UP's control. In January of 1868, the Pacific Pullman Company was formed, with Union Pacific taking 2600 of its 5000 shares. Pullman and Carnegie each received 1200 shares.

The Pullman cars were an immediate success, which further inspired George Pullman to develop the 'Hotel Train.' Dining, drawing room and saloon cars were added to the sleepers. These additions eliminated the need for meal stops, and consequently the travel time was cut back. The 'Hotel Train' ran only for one year, but its short run suggested the luxury of future Union Pacific trains.

Although Pullman cars eased the trip to a degree, travel by train was not without its hardships. Incidents such as a fire in a Cheyenne machine shop and an Indian uprising during which a section hand was killed provided ammunition for the road's detractors and jarred the nerves of the UP's passengers. But perhaps the worst part of the journey was simply fatigue and discomfort. Passengers were faced with long delays between connections in Chicago and across the Missouri River, they endured the freezing tempuratures of winter and the heat of summer, and they were subjected to steak, pototoes, eggs and tea for every meal.

What made the ride a delight was the scenic beauty of the countryside. Travelers watched the landscape change from the rolling plains to the rugged mountains to the starkness of the desert to the lush vegetation of California. Glimpses of prairie dogs, coyotes, wolves, bears, elk, and even buffalo could be seen as the Union Pacific wound its way across the continent. To the citizens from the East these were the sights of a lifetime.

A Time of Great Invention

The years 1870 to 1890 were also responsible for many inventions and improvements greatly beneficial to the railroad industry as a whole, and their usefulness even spilled over to related industries, such as cattle ranching, farming, sheepherding, and mining. Inventions useful to farming included the reaper, the combine, Wheeler's modification of the windmill, the chilled-steel plow and barbed wire. During this period, the number of individual farms in America almost tripled.

Ashbel Welch of the Camden & Amboy Railroad developed a manual block signal system in 1865 after grisly troop train wrecks during the Civil War. Later, in 1872, William Robinson patented an automatic block signal, accomplished by electrifying track circuits, thereby greatly reducing the frequency of accidents and collisions.

In 1868, Confederate veteran Major Eli H Janney patented his automatic coupler and by 1893 it was made madatory equipment for all trains. One year after Janney patented his automatic coupler, George Westinghouse patented the air brake. The Railroad Safety Appliance Act signed by President Benjamin Harrison in March of 1893 also required air brakes on all trains.

Improvements for the Union Pacific

The locomotives of the late nineteenth century, perhaps more than any other invention of the era, became a symbol

Below: **An engraving of the interior of a Pullman sleeper, and a photograph of the same** *(above opposite).* **The berths pulled down for sleeping and folded up for daytime.** *Below right:* **A UP dining car in the 1880s.** *Far right:* **A Union Pacific parlor car in the early 1900s.**

of the times. Its power made possible a journey across the continent, a journey that to an earlier era would have seemed impossible. As the century drew to a close, great strides were made in improving the size and power of locomotives.

In the 1880s and 1890s, technology created new, stronger locomotives able to haul heavier and longer trains. Design modificatons improved both freight and passenger service. Articulated construction allowed the longer locomotive to bend while rounding curves. Better adhesion of wheel to track enabled trains to haul more and improve their overall pulling power. By 1887 locomotives traveling through western blizzards were equipped with a rotary snowplow—an amazing device that proved quite effective against the deep Wyoming snows. The 'Wooten' or 'dirt burner' locomotive experimented with low-grade slack coal from the Wyoming mines. This experiment, however, did not match the success of the rotary snowplow.

The 'American-type' engine, or the 4-4-0, became the most widely used type of locomotive in nineteenth century North America. The Whyte system of numerical classification came into general use about 1900. The first digit refers to the number of wheels in the pilot truck at the front of the engine. The second refers to the number of large driving wheels or drivers, and the third shows the number of wheels, if any, in the trailing truck under the cab.

Below: A steam locomotive charges across the plains—like the buffaloes who populated the plains before the arrival of the Iron Horse.

The Union Pacific Number 1, *General Sherman* was a 4-4-0 'American-type' engine. Union Pacific's famous 4-4-0, Number 119, met the Central Pacific's *Jupiter* at Promontory, Utah for the golden spike ceremony in 1869.

UP *Camel* 768 was built by Rogers Works of Patterson, New Jersey, in 1887. First introduced by B&O engineer and inventor Ross Winans, the camel-back locomotive was so named for the position of the cab, mounted over the boiler and with eight drivers. Rogers produced large numbers of the 4-4-0 locomotive.

Inspired by the great locomotives, Bill Fries, Richard Proulx, and J Berkey composed the Union Pacific theme song, 'A Great Big Rollin' Railroad':

We're a great big rollin' railroad,
hear the diesel engine's power;
we're a thousand wheels of freight train
doin' ninety miles an hour
From the great plains of Nebraska
on to Las Vegas and LA,
From Missouri down through Texas
we've got the right of way.
From the Gulf Coast to St Louis
to the blue Pacific shore,
we'll deliver your great cargo
and come rollin' home for more.
We're America's new railroad,
clear the track, we're coming through.
We're the Union Pacific,
we can handle it for you.
We're the Union Pacific,
we can handle it for you!

The Debt Crisis: The Panic of 1873

During this bright period of invention and growth, a dark, ominous cloud was developing for the railroad industry. Ironically, the problems were a result of the very act that made the first transcontinental railroad possible. The Pacific Railroad Act of 1864 was as vague as the Pacific Railroad Act of 1862. The later act, however, dangled the prospect of improved federal aid but failed to solve the problem of generating funds to get construction underway. Investors

Below: The *General Sherman* was the first locomotive purchased by UP. *At right:* UP 2-8-2 Number 1938, another classic locomotive, was used for local freight and switch work as well as for pusher service on the steep grade of the Missouri River Valley near Omaha.

found that their securities had no market until the road was built and no profits could be expected until it began operating. The only immediate return lay in profits from construction, but these were paid largely in securities of the road. By 1874, three crucial questions spawned by the ambiguities of the Pacific Acts had already found their way into the courts. These questions are paraphrased as follows: When were the interest payments due? When was the road actually completed? How should net earnings be defined?

Western railroad speculation was one of the major contributing factors of the Panic of 1873. The Panic was essentially the result of years of over-expansion, over-production, over-speculation, inflation, inflated paper money and the floating debts existing since the over-capitalization of the early roads. It was affecting all sectors of the economy, and was especially hard on the banks and financial institutions. The failure of Jay Cooke's brokerage house on 18 September 1873, when he couldn't support his debts for Jim Hill's

Northern Pacific Railroad, signaled the beginning of the end. Thirty-eight banks and brokerage houses closed on that ominous day. Two days later, the New York Stock Exchange was closed for an unprecedented 10 days. Over 10,000 businesses would fail before 1880, and 10,478 went bankrupt before the end of the decade.

As eastern businesses collapsed, western railroads failed. Loans were called, capital was impossible to obtain, and government and company securities fell. Construction came to a halt and many lines went into receivership. A consequence of the Panic was a change in the public's view of the railroads, particularly in the West, where numerous railroads failed. Twenty years earlier the railroads had been the source of promise; now they symbolized only hard times.

The Panic of 1873 triggered one of the fiercest industrial rate wars in the history of railroading. It was during this period of decline that Jay Gould assumed control of the Union Pacific.

The UP Under Jay Gould

Jay Gould assumed the presidency of the Union Pacific in 1874. Untrustworthy and a notorious wheeler-dealer, Gould managed to keep Union Pacific afloat, but derived pleasure from pitting one railroad against another in order to beat down its buying price. He amassed almost one-half of all the railroad mileage in the country by 1890, much of which rivaled the lines controlled by the Union Pacific. He was responsible for forcing the Union Pacific into numerous consolidations, the most famous being the merger with the Kansas Pacific. He'd bought control of the Kansas Pacific and the Denver Pacific in 1879, which together formed a route from Kansas City through Denver to Cheyenne that competed with the UP's line from Omaha to Cheyenne.

In 1880, with Dodge as his chief engineer, he pushed the Texas & Pacific toward El Paso and the Gulf of Mexico. After gaining control of the Missouri, Kansas & Texas, he leased it to the Missouri Pacific and announced plans for 600 miles of extensions, including a connection to the Texas & Pacific. On 19 August the Burlington authorized their own Denver extension, which opened in May of 1881. The Denver extension had been a source of contention for the Union Pacific and the Missouri Pacific, which Gould had acquired in 1879. Gould held seats on both railroads and threatened to move the Missouri into Chicago, pull out of Nebraska, and shift its business to rival lines. Gould did not carry out his threats, but he had the reputation of being unpredictable, and seemed to others to act spontaneously without obvious cause.

The Burlington's Denver extension, along with the Rio Grande Western's line to Ogden, created a route that ran parallel to the entire length of the Union Pacific. In answer to the threats from these rival railroads, the UP accelerated its expansion plan and completed a line running from the fork of the Platte River and along the South Platte to a connection with the Denver Pacific. Lines were also initiated from Denver to Longmont, from Fort Collins to North Park and from Loveland Pass to Leadville. Union Pacific's expansion plans extended west into Utah and Nevada, as well as north, into Montana and Oregon.

The Denver extension opened the door to an era of .expansionist wars unprecedented in scale or fury. The consequences were far-reaching and virtually every railroad was left scarred. None, however, suffered more immediate losses than the Union Pacific. Not until Harriman resurrected a new Union Pacific would it once again dominate the continent.

A Few More Words From Grenville Dodge

In February of 1875 Jay Gould, who had become heavily interested in the Union Pacific Railway, in connection with Messrs Ames, Dillon and the Board of Directors, conceived a plan of paying to the government, in addition to the sum it was then receiving from the company, a sum of money each year that should be used as a sinking fund, which, at the maturity of the government bond, would liquidate that indebtedness. The Honorable James F Wilson,

After the Panic of 1873, the railroad industry went into a period of decline, and the UP—under the leadership of Jay Gould—(below), was no exception. Despite those trying times, the UP survived as is evidenced by this twentieth century locomotive.

of Iowa, a government director, and myself were selected to go to Washington to present the matter to the government. General Grant was then President, and General Benjamin F Bristow Secretary of the Treasury.

We presented the proposition to General Grant, who looked upon it favorably and referred it to the Secretary of the Treasury for the purpose of having a bill drawn which would carry out our views. The entire Cabinet was in favor of the proposition with the single exception of Mr Jewell, of Connecticut. Upon the report of General Bristow, General Grant drafted a message to the Congress of the United States recommending the passage of an act that would carry out this plan.

In the meantime, rumors of what we were doing had reached New York, where there was a large, short interest in the stock of the Union Pacific. This interest immediately gathered its forces and influence and sent persons to Washington to represent to the President that the proposed action of the Union Pacific was a mere stock-jobbing scheme for the purpose of manipulating Union Pacific stock, and their representations made such an impression on General Grant that he never sent his message in, and the company, receiving the treatment it did, then abandoned for the time all efforts to make a settlement with the government.

General Grant often said to me in later years that he regretted that he did not settle the matter at that time. This demonstrates that, at the moment the Union Pacific began to be prosperous, the men who put their money in it and built it made the first effort to pay the debt due the government at or before its maturity. If their offer had been accepted, the earnings of the company demonstrated that they would have been able to have met their agreement, and at the maturity of the debt it would have been paid.

This is one of the many instances in which the Union Pacific Railway has endeavored to fulfill, not only in letter, but in spirit as well, every obligation it owed to the government, and I undertake to say that the government of the United States, from the time the road was finally completed and in continuous operation, has never fulfilled any one of its obligations to the company, except the simple giving of its credit at the time of the building by the issue of its bonds.
—Grenville Dodge

Gould belonged to a new type of 'mobile businessman.' While board members, like Forbes, closely allied the corporation with individuals, Gould recognized that corporations outlived their founders and, as circumstances changed, so did the interests of the individual. Gould kept railroad executives guessing as to his next move, particularly

during the year 1879. He had inflated the value of two smaller roads and forced Union Pacific to consolidate with them through an exchange of stock.

The Central Branch and Kansas Central ultimately proved of little value, but the St Joseph properties, after a slow start, prospered as part of a short line to St Louis. He bought control of the Kansas Pacific in 1879, and again muscled the board of directors of UP to exchange stock at par— 'notwithstanding the fact that Kansas Pacific stock was earning nothing while Union Pacific was earning and paying six percent per annum,' and UP was selling for $60 a share while Kansas Pacific was a mere $13 a share. Gould and his friends were buying up Kansas Pacific stock at the low rate in order to make a killing when the consolidation was announced. In 1887, before the Pacific Railway Commis-

sion hearings, Gould said that the UP directors insisted on the merger and that he had offered to back out. Could they have logically done otherwise? If they had refused to Gould's terms for the merger, he would carry out his plan to extend his system to the shores of the Pacific Ocean by connecting the Kansas Pacific to the Central Pacific at Salt Lake City, ultimately destroying the Union Pacific. Gould also added the Western Pacific to his list of controlled roads in 1879. All the while the members of the Union Pacific executive board continued to believe that his loyalties lay with the Union Pacific.

At left: The Union Pacific Railroad at Weber Canyon, Utah in the 1870s— when Gould was exploiting the railroad. *Below:* An 1870 wood engraving depicting an elegant dining car on the Union Pacific. Dining cars proved to be expensive and were temporarily eliminated from 1881-88.

Below: These reproductions of the Union Pacific's Number 119 and Central Pacific's *Jupiter* reenact the historic meeting at Promontory, Utah on 10 May 1869.

Although the consolidation was blamed for the financial difficulties of the eighties, it turned out far better than anyone might have expected. Buying rival lines as an act of self-defense had already become standard practice among American railroads by 1880. But pitting them one against the other in a fight to the death was a practice Gould had pioneered. Far from being a disaster, the consolidation averted a dangerous situation that most certainly would have developed had the Kansas Pacific been a competitor during the rate wars of the next decade. Finally, the Kansas Pacific and the Denver Pacific both remain an integral part of the Union Pacific today.

Early in 1881 Gould's intentions became clear. He was building a new system in the Southwest. By April of 1882 Gould had withdrawn entirely from an active role in Union Pacific affairs, although he kept his seat on the executive committee. About that time he gained control of Western Union Telegraph Company and had a controlling interest in New York Elevated Railways. From 1879 to 1883 he owned the *New York World*. By 1890, he controlled almost one half of all the railway mileage in the Southwestern United States, owning the Missouri Pacific, Texas & Pacific, St Louis, Southwestern, and the International & Great Northern.

At his death, in December of 1892, few people had anything good to say about him. Even the stock market didn't waver. Ironically, his stocks were up. 'No harder judgment,' wrote Burton J Hendrick in the *American Illustrated Magazine* a few months later, 'was ever passed upon a departed millionaire.' The newspapers ran obituaries that held Gould in the highest contempt and blamed him for the deprivation of the entire society.

The *New York Herald* wrote, 'His financial success, judged by the means by which it was attained, is not to be envied. His great wealth was purchased at too high a price.'

From the *New York Times*, '...Gould was a negative quantity in the development of the country where he was not an absolutely retarding and destructive quantity.'

Finally, from the paper he owned for five years, comes the harshest criticsm of all, 'Jails, insane asylums and almshouses all over the land are peopled with those who

aspired to wealth by similar methods, and with their victims. These are but a fraction of those who have been corrupted and morally ruined. The majority are at large, mingling with the community in all the walks of life, excusing, practicing, and disseminating the vices of which he was the most conspicuous model in modern times.'

One can say Gould was a good family man. He left his family well provided for after his death, and divided his estate equally between his six children. Unfortunately, the heir to his railroad empire, his eldest son George, lacked the intelligence and drive of his father. In 1927 he was ousted by his siblings as chief executor and trustee of the estate. His career as 'a great railroad magnate' cost the estate upwards of $25,000,000.

The Interstate Commerce Commission

In 1881, the Supreme Court reversed an earlier decision and ruled that a state could not regulate rates on shipments passing beyond its own borders. Public outcry over the unfair advantage given to large city freight traffic over small Western towns, and the apparent lack of interest in providing passenger service, gave rise to the 'Granger laws' and 'Granger decisions' which preceded the Interstate Commerce Act. Originally the Grangers were a social organization promoting the principles of education and fellowship. Their grassroots structure enabled them to take an active stand against the railroads and lobby Congress for help. Granger laws were passed in many states, but no federal effort to control the railroads was made until 1887.

On 4 February 1887 the Interstate Commerce Act was signed into law by President Grover Cleveland, thereby establishing the Interstate Commerce Commission (ICC). The federal agency was committed to eliminating the railroad practices of giving rebates to favored shippers and of imposing higher charges for noncompetitive hauls. Despite the high ideals put forth by the ICC, it lacked any real enforcement ability. Minor adjustments were made through the passage of the Elkins Act in 1903, prohibiting rebates. However, it was not until 1906 and the passage of the Hepburn Act that a much strengthened ICC was able to effect any change. This Act increased the size of the ICC to

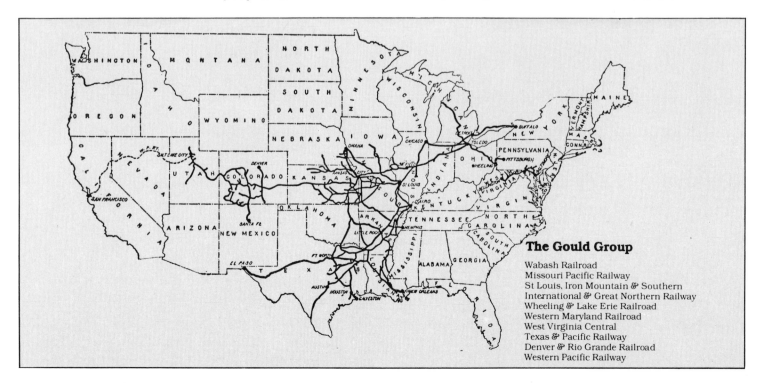

The Gould Group

Wabash Railroad
Missouri Pacific Railway
St Louis, Iron Mountain & Southern
International & Great Northern Railway
Wheeling & Lake Erie Railroad
Western Maryland Railroad
West Virginia Central
Texas & Pacific Railway
Denver & Rio Grande Railroad
Western Pacific Railway

The map *at left* shows Jay Gould's empire in 1892. Points along this line, as they appear today—Green River, Wyoming, where the Mormons once lent their assistance *(above)*; the station at Topeka, Kansas *(below)*; and the station at historic Medicine Bow, Wyoming *(at bottom)*.

seven members and extended its authority over express. sleeping-car and pipeline companies. In addition, the Hepburn Act strengthened the regulations against rebates. prohibited free passes (except for railroad employees and hardship cases) and, most importantly, gave the ICC power to establish 'just and reasonable' maximum rates. In spite of the changes it created, many liberals were dissatified with the Hepburn Act because it still allowed the courts to reverse, or at the very least delay, ICC orders.

An Era of Regulation

Improved safety and the standardization of the railroad industry was another result of regulation. By 1883, railroads covered ground between both coasts on regular schedules. As could be expected, difficulty arose when accurate time-tables could not be produced. Railroads put an end to the confusion by dividing the country into four time zones. It was not accepted by the public until 1918, when Congress passed the Standard Time Act and made the four time zones official. Due to the number of interconnecting railroads across the nation, the need for a standard track gauge became apparent. The time it took to transfer freight to the odd gauged track was costly and the rate wars were in full swing. By 1886 most railroads had shifted to the narrow gauge, measuring four feet, eight and one-half inches, the standard for all Union Pacific rails. In 1893 President Benjamin Harrison signed the Safety Appliance Act, making air brakes and automatic couplers mandatory on all trains.

The Presidency of Charles Francis Adams, Jr

I n 1884 Charles Francis Adams took the reigns of the Union Pacific Railroad during its period of decline. It was not an easy position for anyone to be in, let alone for someone who had acquired the title of expert by writing a few articles and publishing a book on the nature of the railroads, and not by actually working his way up through the ranks. His experience and personality made him unlike any other rail executive before him. He came into the railroad industry at the top and viewed with contempt those who had come in at the bottom and worked their way up. He sat on the Massachusetts Railroad Commission in 1869 and recorded that experience in his book *Railroads, Their Origins and Problems*. That book, in addition to a series of articles on the state of the railroads, established him as an expert the subject. He occupied a post with Union Pacific as an arbitrator, and he was encouraged to sit on the board of Union Pacific during its most unstable period in the 1880s. The old guard saw in Adams a glimmer of hope. It seemed that they'd tried everything and had had enough of Gould and what was generally perceived as backstabbing. Adams prided himself on being an intellectual, and had a vision of a new Union Pacific improved by better management personnel. Adams was openly inviting the press and the people to examine his procedures, contrasting his way with the corrupt practices of Gould. The press loved the good/evil distinction drawn between the two and Adams encouraged

In 1888, Charles Adams spent $3.1 million on improvements for the Union Pacific, including locomotives, box cars and sleepers. *Below:* **A sleeper as portrayed by** *The Saturday Evening Post.* *Right:* **A club car appointed with comfortable leather chairs and spittoons.**

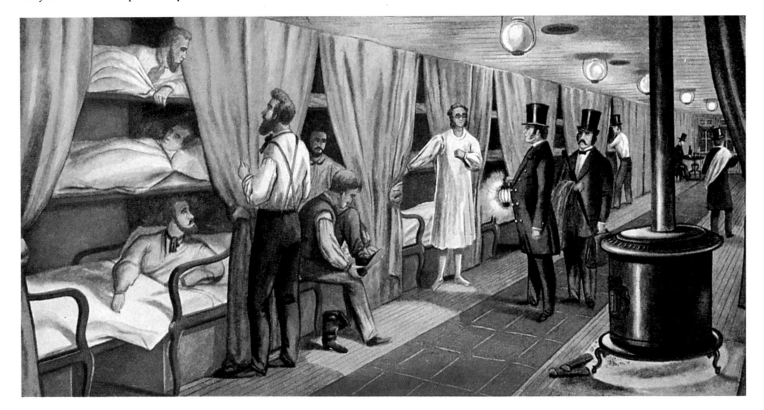

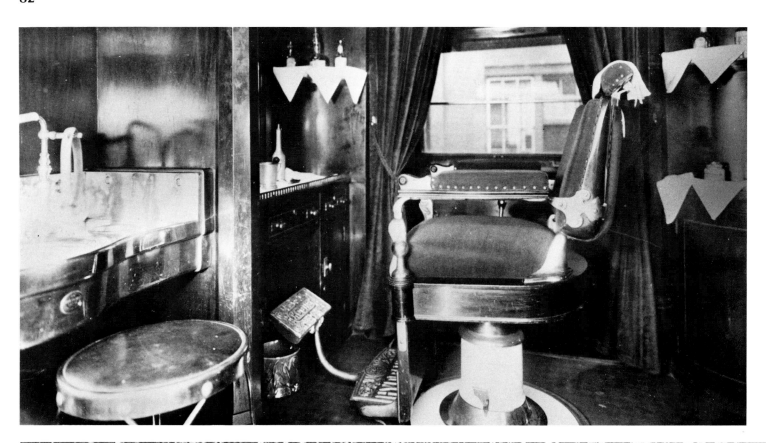

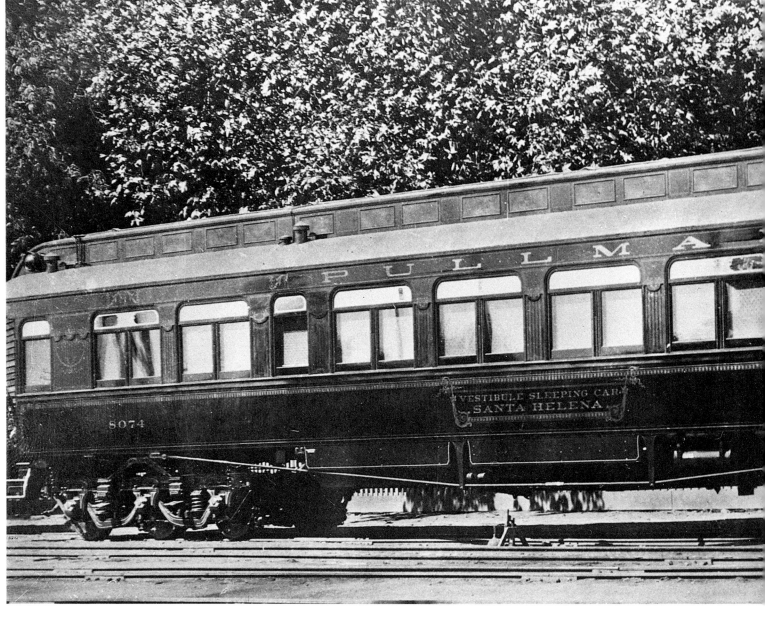

it. Even critics in June of 1884 recognized the immense challenge facing him, and were content to wait and watch before attacking his revolutionary ideas.

During this time, Union Pacific's floating debt was still on the rise. As President, Adams lacked the experience of railroad men who had worked their way up from the bottom. Armed mostly with book-learning, Adams proved to be a risk-taker, hoping to make theory into practice. By August of 1886 it paid off. In selling the Grand Island line at an unreasonably low price, he managed to make enough profit to alleviate the entire floating debt. Ironically, one month later he was swept into the war of expansion and pursued routes in the Far West with Grenville Dodge, leaving other railroads to haggle over routes to Chicago.

Early in 1886 rate wars flared up among passenger lines and soon spread to freight service as well. Although rate wars raged throughout the country, most focused on the St Louis-Chicago corridor and the major East Coast ports. In desperation, railroads were trying to expand their lines and improve services to attract customers in an attempt to salvage their sinking stocks. To answer the demand for

Below: **A typical Pullman sleeper car of the late nineteenth century. Other Pullman innovations included the on-train barber shop at *left* as well as dining cars. The UP's Charles Adams purchased 13 diners from the Pullman Company during the 'Great Dining Car War of 1888–89.'**

improved service Adams started a new train, the *Overland Flyer*, which ran from Omaha to San Francisco in 71 hours and to Portland in 77 hours. During the first four months of service, the *Flyer* used both coach cars and Pullman sleepers, but then switched to only Pullmans to ensure higher quality. Adams also attempted to improve the quality of meal stops by leasing the eating houses to the men who ran the Millard House in Omaha.

Dining cars, though effective in shortening routes, proved to be too costly a solution, so in 1881 the UP, the Atchison and the Burlington had signed an agreement not to use them. In 1887 Northern Pacific put a diner on its Portland train, causing Adams' subordinates to urge him to do the same. Adams finally agreed and was soon entangled in the Great Dining Car War of 1888-89. Ultimately, UP purchased 13 diners from the Pullman Company. The demand for larger and more rolling stock continued to come from Adams' directors on all sides. Adams estimated that since the diversification in types of traffic had grown so great, the Union Pacific would need new equipment to upgrade the lines. In 1888 he spent over $3.1 million on locomotives, box cars, flat cars, stock cars, coal cars, fruit cars, refrigerator cars, dump cars, furniture cars, chair cars, diners, Pullman sleepers, emigrant sleepers, baggage cars, and express and mail cars. Because other lines followed suit, no one gained

84

the advantage, the end result being higher costs without profits.

Passes, another necessary evil of the railroads, took their toll on the Union Pacific. Typical figures for a month in 1892 saw the distribution of 4985 trip passes to 8133 customers, plus $35,940 in unclassified time passes totalling $88,922 in free transportation by the Union Pacific.

As a source of fuel and traffic, coal was a vital asset to any railroad company. But to the Union Pacific, whose lines went through the heart of the mining lands, control of coal production was essential. When Adams took office the Colorado holdings were swept together into the Union Coal Company, the result of numerous court battles over the ownership of the mines along the railroads. The Court finally decided in favor of Union Pacific. Despite a successful first year under Adams' administration, the mines were becoming less efficient and more costly to operate. Adams was faced with three possible options: he could abandon the coal business altogether; he could deliver it to outside parties and maintain limited involvement as a figurehead; or he could reorganize it and continue working it in its new form. With the help of Mark Hanna, Adams' primary source on coal issues, a solution to the coal problem came in the form of a subsidiary, Union Pacific Coal Company, in 1890. It was welcomed as the first UP subsidiary and the first step in creating an auxilliary network of resources crucial to the future prosperity of the road. In addition to expanding the coal operations, Adams explored the tourist trade. Although he was never able to complete the idea, Adams considered running a branch to Yellowstone Park. Adams understood that the value of Union Pacific went far beyond its function as a carrier, but he was a man ahead of his times and unable to solve the pressing problems of the day.

Despite all his efforts, Adams was never able to resolve the government debt. The rate wars had kept the industry, and Union Pacific, in debt. After six years at the helm, Adams resigned and Gould resumed control.

Coal has always been a source traffic for the UP. *Below:* A western coal mine at about the turn of the century. *At right:* A modern-day Union Pacific coal train 'loading up' at the Prospect Point Mine.

THE ROCK SPRINGS MASSACRE

White miners in Wyoming resented the introduction of Chinese miners to their mines and the raises given to miners in Colorado. In January of 1885 the miners in Carbon, Wyoming struck. The pay inequity was righted, but still the wages weren't enough. The labor situation was complicated by the fact that in 1875 the Union Pacific had contracted Beckwith and Quinn to provide all the labor for the mines. It evolved into an agreement whereby they, acting as agents for the company, would hire Chinese labor and pay the white miners. Grievances against the Chinese miners ranged from preferred treatment in receiving specialty foods, to keeping the wage of white miners artificially low. The labor situation worsened steadily until there was a threat of a general strike. The most unstable spot was Rock Springs, Colorado.

What began as an isolated incident between a pair of white miners and two Chinese miners in Mine Number Six developed quickly into a mob of white miners storming into Chinatown, shooting as they went, and burning to the ground 100 homes. The most unsettling aspect of the ugly scene, uncovered by journalist Isaac Bromley, was that although the crowd had given the Chinese an hour to leave town, while they were hurriedly collecting their belongings and before even one-half an hour had passed, the mob suddenly opened fire on the Chinese and looted their houses before setting them ablaze. Bromley's reportage convinced Adams that the Company was 'fully responsible for the employment of the Chinese,' and that something had

to be done quickly, in a forceful and even violent manner. Below is an excerpt of Adams' reasoning:

'Anything which brings about a remedy has got to be radical in its character. It is useless to talk of quelling these men, or of dismissing them. It cannot be done. They constitute almost the entire region in which our road is operated. They are at present thoroughly demoralized. We have got to meet them squarely and educate them…A condition of paralysis cannot continue long and when the explosion has taken place I am strongly inclined to believe that the better portion of our employees will gradually assert themselves over the worst portion. Under proper rules and regulations the weeding out process might be entered upon. We can get rid of the drunken, the immoral and the dishonest.'

No explosion ever came that enabled Adams to install an enlightened policy for relations between management and labor. Far ahead of his time, Adams' visionary proposal was detailed and highly stratified, covering the distinction between permanent and temporary employes, job security, seniority, regular pay increases, benefits, hospitalization, retirement pensions, illness or disability pensions, accident or death insurance, and education for the children of company employes. Adams knew that none of it could work unless labor had a voice. The thought of granting representation privileges to the workers made his officers, the 'practical' railroad men, quake in their boots. All of them viewed shared power as a threat to their authority, and Adams dropped the issue. In 1889 he had his treatise published but nothing came of it. Not until decades later would his program be implemented in its entirety, dispelling the notion that 'What has been, is, and will always be.'

UP President Adams had to deal with angry coal miners. Colorado miners (opposite and below) resented their Chinese coworkers because cheap Chinese labor kept wages low.

The Harriman Era

I n 1893 the country was plunged into another depression, but this time Union Pacific did not fare as well. During the Panic of 1893 the Union Pacific went bankrupt and went into receivership. It was sold in 1897 to Edward H Harriman, a shrewd railroad tycoon and President of the Illinois Central. As a director of UP, Harriman launched a $25 million campaign, and within two years, despite the fact that loadings had declined 15 percent, he had doubled earnings and made Union Pacific the finest railroad in the United States. In 1900, after the death of Collis Huntington, the last of the Big Four, Harriman was issued $100,000,000 of convertible Union Pacific bonds to 'use as his judgment may be practicable and desireable.' Harriman used the funds to buy up Huntington's stock in the Southern Pacific, giving the Union Pacific 46 percent of the Southern Pacific and ownership of the Central Pacific. He then set to work updating and improving the SP and saw to the completion of three projects. First, he ordered the straightening of a 10-mile stretch of track between San Francisco and Los Angeles, eliminating a steeply graded inland route in favor of a coastal route. Next, he ordered the construction of a 60-mile cutoff between Burbank and Montalvo in Southern California. His final and most costly time-saving project was the Lucin Cutoff across the Great Salt Lake in Utah. By the project's completion, Harriman had shaved 44 miles off the old route north of Salt Lake, including the original transcontinental line at Promontory. In 1903 he became President of the Union Pacific and began buying stocks in railroads across the country, establishing a rail network that would interface with the Union Pacific.

Although much of the new track mileage constructed during the early years of the twentieth century added branch lines to existing routes, four new construction projects were completed by 1912. Three of the new lines were located in the West, the fourth in Florida. Of the three lines in the West, two challenged Harriman's empire at Union Pacific.

The San Pedro, Los Angeles & Salt Lake Railroad

Late in 1900 William A Clark, a Montana copper magnate, announced plans to build a line from Los Angeles to Salt Lake City, a route which would compete with Harriman's California traffic. Clark had come West in 1863 as a young man seeking a fortune in gold. Though he never found gold, he did find success as a tobacco merchant, later turned to banking and investing, and finally to politics.

To stop Clark, Harriman gave the orders to renew work on an abandoned extension that ran through a Nevada

canyon called the Meadow Valley Wash. Rival crews from Clark's San Pedro, Los Angeles & Salt Lake Railroad and Harriman's Union Pacific were soon facing off in this narrow and strategic gorge. Armed with barbed wire, tree stumps and log barricades, the competing gangs did what they could to slow each other's progess until the battle finally moved into the courts. Following extensive litigation, the parties reached an agreement stating that Clark and Harriman would jointly control the San Pedro line. Once completed, the 775-mile line added a new route for mineral traffic and helped speed the transfer of California fruits and vegetables to the tables of the East. Harriman celebrated his success by launching a new passenger train, the *Los Angeles Limited.*

At right: **Railroad tycoon Edward H Harriman purchased the bankrupt Union Pacific in 1897, and within two years returned it to prosperity, making the UP the finest railroad in the United States.**

Los Angeles Limited: 'The Train Delux of the West'

The following is an excerpt from Union Pacific's 1905 brochure describing the *Los Angeles Limited.*

The *Los Angeles Limited,* running daily between Los Angeles and Chicago, traverses a country rich in historic interest as well as pictorial beauty.

From Los Angeles to Salt Lake City the journey is over the Salt Lake Route, traversing the states of California, Nevada and Utah, each with many scenes of beauty and novelty for the entertainment of the traveler. From Salt Lake City to Omaha, Northern Utah, Wyoming and Nebraska are crossed via the Union Pacific Railroad. Beyond Omaha, through Iowa and Illinois, the Chicago and Northwestern Railway takes the train over the only double track railroad in the West.

...The service has been given special attention, and only capable and courteous men are employed. The daily newspapers of the various cities will be found on all the trains of the *Los Angeles Limited,* as well as a telegraphic bulletin furnishing a digest of the world's various new items.

The train and all that pertains to it has been built with an idea of furnishing passengers to and from California the highest degree of perfection in railroad traveling. This idea has been fully realized, as the popularity of this train will now bear witness.

At right: A map of the Union Pacific system during the Harriman era and a Southern Pacific ticket *(above)* from the same time period. Harriman gained control of the Southern Pacific in 1900.

The Battle with Western Pacific Railway

Harriman did not fare as well in his battle with the Western Pacific Railway, a road that would connect Salt Lake City, Utah with Oakland, California. Harriman hindered work on the road by charging exorbitant rates for delivery of construction materials needed by Western Pacific. Though never proven, it was suspected that Harriman's people stirred up trouble among the WP workers. It has also been said that Union Pacific lured away Western Pacific workers with the promise of high wages and then fired the new recruits. In addition, Southern Pacific tried to keep Western Pacific out of the San Francisco Bay at Oakland. In spite of Harriman and Southern Pacific, Western Pacific obtained its terminal on the harbor and completed the line.

The Northern Securities Company

During Harriman's tenure at UP, rival railroad executive and financier Jim Hill founded the Northern Securities Company. Together with Harriman and JP Morgan, they controlled the bulk of the northern roads. This maneuver was found by the ICC to be incongruous with the Sherman Antitrust Act of 1890, and in 1904 the Supreme Court ruled that the Northern Securities Company be dissolved. Subsequent Court decisions gave Hill full control over the main lines. Unable to wield any influence over northern lines, Harriman sold his stock. By 1906 the ICC discovered Harriman's use of the Union Pacific as a holding company for the stock of other companies and, after an investigation, reported it to be not in the public's interest.

Harriman and President Roosevelt

In November of 1906 President Theodore Roosevelt ordered the ICC to investigate Edward H Harriman's railroad empire as part of his campaign against Big Business. What looked to the nation to be a case of the President making an example of a monopolist was actually Theodore Roosevelt taking out a personal grudge against Harriman. Once friends, the estrangement between Roosevelt and Harriman resulted from the nonpayment of an old debt. When Harriman and the Southern Pacific were called upon for help in 1906 after the earthquake and subsequent fire devastated San Francisco, Harriman absorbed the cost for evacuating 224,000 refugees out of the city and delivering 1600 carloads of food and supplies to the needy. Again when the Colorado River overflowed its banks and flooding threatened to destroy the agricultural economy of the

Imperial Valley, Harriman came to the rescue. Finally, when Harriman sent the government a bill for the expenses and labor, Theodore Roosevelt refused to pay. President Roosevelt said that Harriman's gesture was appreciated, but expected as the due from any citizen during the country's time of need. His refusal was borne out of the resentment

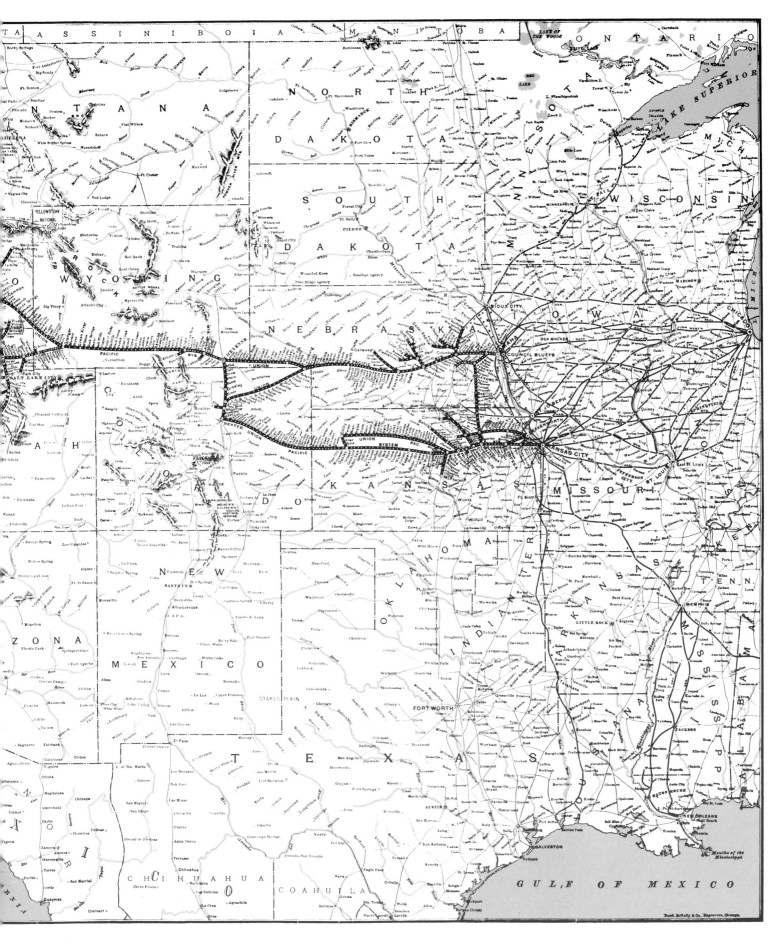

Roosevelt felt when Harriman refused to contribute to his campaign fund. We can speculate that Roosevelt's choice to investigate Harriman's activities in 1906 was an attempt to deter Harriman from pursuing the issue of the debt. That Roosevelt launched attacks on the Union Pacific, the Southern Pacific, the Illinois Central and the Chicago & Alton Railroad's reorganization in 1899 made it obvious that Harriman was a target. By March of 1907, however, all reports of mismanagement on Harriman's lines were found to be invalid. Although Harriman lost popularity among the Washington crowd, the people whose lives he saved had a longer memory and considered Harriman not a criminal, but

THE WESTERN PACIFIC RAILROAD COMPANY

INCORPORATED UNDER THE LAWS OF THE STATE OF CALIFORNIA
THIS CERTIFICATE IS TRANSFERABLE IN THE CITY OF NEW YORK OR IN THE CITY OF SAN FRANCISCO

This certifies that   SALOMON BROS. & HUTZLER   is the owner of

ONE HUNDRED

FULLY PAID AND NON-ASSESSABLE SHARES OF COMMON STOCK WITHOUT PAR VALUE OF THE WESTERN PACIFIC RAILROAD COMPANY

Dated   APR 1 - 1952

SECRETARY

PRESIDENT

Harriman was unsuccessful in his attempt to buy a controlling interest in the Western Pacific. *Above, left and right:* **Western Pacific common stock and preferred stock. Railroads at work in the late nineteenth century—a logging train** *(below right)* **on its run from Oregon to California and a switcher locomotive** *(overleaf)* **at a dock facility. Contrast these western scenes with the elegant UP-SP London Galleries Exhibition** *(inset)* **of 1909.**

the great railroad financier and responsible manager that he was.

President Roosevelt showed obvious favoritism when he allowed multimillionaire JP Morgan's United Steel Corporation to annex the Tennessee Coal & Iron Company. (JP Morgan did contribute to Roosevelt's campaign). Instead of revitalizing small business by making it possible for steel companies to compete in a free market, the net consequence of Theodore Roosevelt's campaign against trusts was the destruction of the existing steel corporations. The end of Roosevelt's years in the White House marked the end of the age of great capitalists.

Between 1901 and his death in 1909, Harriman spent over $240 million improving the Union Pacific system. Under Harriman's leadership, the Southern Pacific gained the respect of the nation during two great natural disasters of the twentieth century (the Colorado River project and the 1906 earthquake that devastated San Francisco). Despite Harriman's contributions to the railroad industry as a whole, the Supreme Court ruled in 1913 that the Union Pacific had to divest itself of all Southern Pacific stock, and the two railroads were separated, becoming rivals once again. By 1923, however, Congress had grown more sympathetic to mergers and let Southern Pacific retain control of its Central Pacific stock.

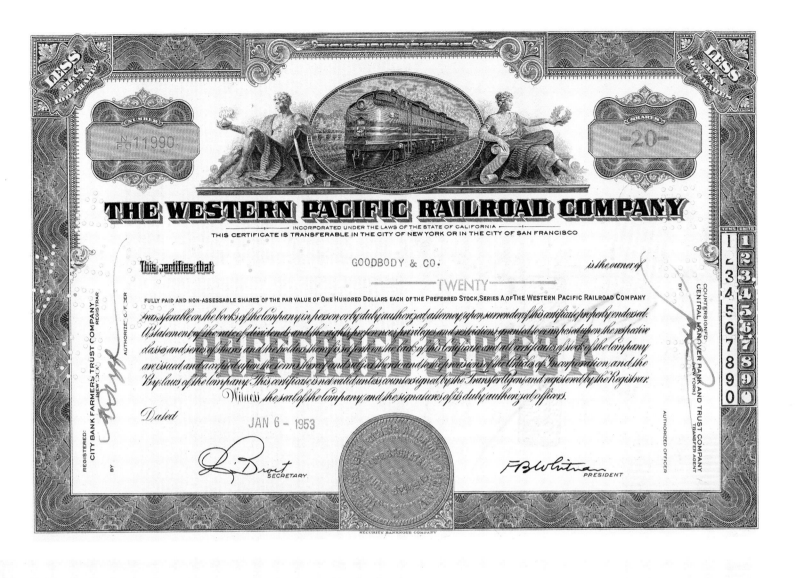

THE WESTERN PACIFIC RAILROAD COMPANY

INCORPORATED UNDER THE LAWS OF THE STATE OF CALIFORNIA

THIS CERTIFICATE IS TRANSFERABLE IN THE CITY OF NEW YORK OR IN THE CITY OF SAN FRANCISCO

NUMBER
NPO 11990

SHARES
-20-

This certifies that   GOODBODY & CO.   is the owner of

TWENTY

FULLY PAID AND NON-ASSESSABLE SHARES OF THE PAR VALUE OF One Hundred Dollars EACH OF THE Preferred Stock, Series A, of The Western Pacific Railroad Company

PREFERRED SERIES A

Dated   JAN 6 - 1953

SECRETARY

PRESIDENT

REGISTERED:
CITY BANK FARMERS TRUST COMPANY
NEW YORK
REGISTRAR
BY
AUTHORIZED OFFICER

COUNTERSIGNED
CENTRAL HANOVER BANK AND TRUST COMPANY
NEW YORK
TRANSFER AGENT
BY
AUTHORIZED OFFICER

SECURITY BANKNOTE COMPANY

The Early Twentieth Century

In the early years of the twentieth century, nearly 50,000 miles of new track were laid, bringing the grand total of track across the country to nearly 225,000 miles in 1906. Nearly two-thirds of this mileage was controlled by the following seven groups:

1) The Harriman system, 25,000 miles, managed by Edward H Harriman, consisting mainly of the Union Pacific, the Southern Pacific, and the Illinois Central. After assuming control of the UP, one of Harriman's first efforts was to regain the branch lines lost during the receivership. He had also gained control of Southern Pacific, which at this time consisted of what was once the Central Pacific and the Western Pacific (no relation to the later railroad of that name). The line ran from Oregon, through California, across Arizona, New Mexico and Texas, terminating at New Orleans. Branch extensions ran through Nevada to Ogden, Utah and from Brownsville to Denison, Texas. The Illinois Central ran from Chicago to New Orleans, with extensions to Sioux Falls, South Dakota; Madison, Wisconsin; St Louis, Missouri and Omaha, Nebraska.

2) The Vanderbilt roads, 22,500 miles, created by Commodore Cornelius Vanderbilt and managed by his heirs, including the New York Central lines and the Chicago & Northwestern.

3) The Hill roads, 21,000 miles, controlled by Jim Hill—Harriman's rival during the fight for control of northern routes. The Hill roads included the Northern Pacific, the Great Northern, and the Burlington.

4) The Pennsylvania group, 20,000 miles, including the Chesapeake & Ohio and the Baltimore & Ohio, in addition to the parent line, the Pennsylvania.

5) The Morgan roads, 18,000 miles, dominated by JP Morgan, including the Southern and the Erie, along with many small southern lines.

6) The Gould roads, 17,000 miles, run by George J Gould, son of Jay Gould, including the Missouri Pacific, plus other roads in the West and Southwest. As has been noted elsewhere in this text, George Gould tangled with Harriman and the Union Pacific in a battle over the Western Pacific, which ran from Salt Lake City, Utah to Oakland, California.

7) The Rock Island system, 15,000 miles, created by William H Moore, including much mileage in the Mississippi Valley in addition to the Rock Island.

Railroad construction slowed considerably during the second decade of the twentieth century. Rail mileage did reach an all-time high of 254,037 miles by 1916, but the total had decreased to 240,293 miles by 1920. The decline in construction was due in part to the introduction of interurban electric lines, located primarily east of the Mississippi and north of the Ohio River. Construction also declined as the country found itself more and more preoccupied with the fear of war.

World War I

On the eve of World War I the railroad industry faced several problems. Labor disputes came to a head in the summer of 1916, and a strike was scheduled for September. President Woodrow Wilson, sympathetic to labor demands, averted the strike by introducing the Adamson Act, to be effective on 1 January 1917. Through it labor was guaranteed an eight-hour workday, and won a Supreme Court battle against the railroads when employers refused to pay the higher wage costs. The railroads asked for higher rates, as freight rates were not rising with the costs of labor, but the ICC responded with only small increases and these were often delayed.

In addition to the labor crisis, the railroads were confronting the problems of increased wartime traffic. Although the US was not yet directly involved in the war, the country did supply the Allies with military supplies and food. The railroads moved these supplies to the eastern seaboard for shipment across the Atlantic. However, as the war rail traffic moved eastward, unloaded freight cars began to pile up. The Merchant Marine had too few ships and could not move the huge quantities of freight across the ocean. Thus, hundreds of full freight cars were left parked on sidings at the Eastern docks.

In response to the war emergency, the railroads united to form one national rail network under the direction of a Railroads' War Board. The Board was formed specifically to deal with situations such as the traffic problem, and in fact was successfully dealing with the problem when the US entered the war. This voluntary unification was signed by the chief executives of each railroad, and was organized

At right: UP yard switcher 4466 was photographed in Sacramento in 1984—its crew and other personnel discuss the vagaries of traffic in a manner probably similar to their counterparts of the World War I era.

under a resolution motivated partly by genuine patriotism and partly by the desire of many railroad executives to demonstrate to the American public that American railroads under private ownership and control could first and foremost satisfy the demands of the Army and Navy—and, while seeing to the needs of the other branches of government, impose a minimum of hardship upon the civilian population. At the heart of this voluntary unification was the issue of ownership and control of the nation's railroads.

The railroads no longer stood in good favor with the American public and many citizens were in favor of government control over the railroad industry after witnessing England's governmental assumption of railroad operations in 1916. This feeling, coupled with a long-standing governmental distrust, prompted President Woodrow Wilson to quash the autonomous Railroads' War Board in spite of the Board's success: freight tonnage rose from 365 billion in 1916 to 394 billion tons moved in late 1917. President Wilson took over the operation of the railroads on 26 December 1917 and appointed William G McAdoo, Secretary of the Treasury, to be Director General of Railroads.

Through a variety of cost-cutting measures, McAdoo managed to reduce the crisis by the spring of 1918. Duplicate passenger trains were eliminated, sleeping-car service reduced, repair shops were shared and timetables and stations were combined. New controls were added for freight and direct routing prevailed where possible. Some $380 million was spent on restorations and new equipment, including 100,000 freight cars and 1930 locomotives.

However, McAdoo's solutions would create problems for the railroads later on. When the war was over, the railroads were left to cover the expenses incurred for improvements, as well as the pay increases instituted by by the government. In the 26 months of government operation, operating costs exceeded total revenues by $900,000,000. The Union Pacific and the rest of the railroad industry found itself once again in dire straits.

When the war was over, President Woodrow Wilson urged Congress to give serious consideration to the future of American railroads. Although there was some support for the continuation of government control, Congress and public opinion favored a return to private ownership. In March of 1920 the railroads were returned to civilian life.

The Transportation Act of 1920

The Transportation Act of 1920, drafted under the administration of President Warren G Harding, gave the ICC authority in virtually every area of railroading: rates and services, routing of freight, extensions, abandonments and consolidation of lines, and joint use of terminals and equipment. By eliminating disparity in earning power between the powerful and weak carriers, it set the scene for the consolidations and mergers that would change American railroading for the rest of the twentieth century.

Below: The Union Pacific Terminal in Los Angeles, California in the late 1920s. Despite the railroad industry's problems with labor, passenger service continued to thrive. The photograph *at right* illustrates some of the comforts of rail travel in the late 1920s.

The Years Between the World Wars

The Industry Declines

The decline of the railroad industry parallels the rise of the auto industry. When the first automobiles were produced in the early twentieth century, the American public viewed them as a plaything for the wealthy, something akin to playing golf or wearing a wristwatch. Henry Ford, however, changed the face of the auto industry with the advent of his Model T. By 1927 the price of the Model T had gone down from $825 to $260. Everyone owned a Ford. Workers used them to commute to jobs in the city; farmers used them to haul produce to market. As a consequence of the availability of the automobile, the government put more energy and funds into improving the roads of America. The auto increasingly became the preferred method of transportation, and the railroad industry suffered.

An additional hindrance to the railroad industry was the bus. During the 1920s more and more people turned to the motorbus for short trips. Travel by bus was clean and convenient as well as inexpensive, for competition between hundreds and, eventually, thousands of small bus companies kept the fares reasonable. Bus companies merged and began to offer service over longer distances. In the 1920s and 1930s hundreds of small towns had no railroad service. The people of these communities found themselves in need of a new form of transporation between cities. Buses filled the void.

The emerging trucking industry also took business away from the railroads. The smaller size of the vehicle to be filled proved to more economical for a number of businesses. As a result, the railroads shipped less and less uncrated furniture, animals and animal products, milk, and garden produce.

Commercial airlines, which developed in the early twentieth century, were a source of new competition for the railroad industry. Although considered unsafe by some, the speed of air travel outweighed its potential hazards.

The railroads also found themselves competing with old rivals—waterways and pipelines. Both provided economical transportation of freight for much of the East Coast and Midwest.

The Push for Increased Efficiency

Although the years following World War I were indeed years of decline, they were also years of increased operating efficiency. In the early 1920s railroads and shippers joined forces to make railroad transportation more efficient. The Northwest Shippers Advisory Board was established in Minneapolis in 1923 to estimate the area's future railroad needs. Because the Board was so successful, the country was divided into 13 regions, each one governed by its own Shipping Advisory Board.

In the 1930s, the UP introduced such luxurious streamliners as the City of Los Angeles, seen in the advertisement *below. At right:* This high speed diesel was built for the famous streamliner trains.

Charm is expressed in the tastefully appointed interiors of Club and Dining cars . . . in the unobtrusive, courteous service you will find on the Union Pacific

Streamliners

"CITY OF LOS ANGELES" • "CITY OF SAN FRANCISCO" • "CITY OF PORTLAND"

These smart Streamliners provide modern rail service between Chicago and the West Coast. Pullman accommodations and reserved Coach seats.
"CITY OF DENVER" Streamliner . . . overnight service between Chicago and Denver. Pullmans and reserved Coach seats.
Write for free, attractive booklets—California and Pacific Northwest. Address requests to Room 296, Union Pacific Railroad, Omaha, Nebr.

UNION PACIFIC RAILROAD

In that same year, railroad executives met in New York to discuss methods for improving efficiency. Four objectives were agreed upon: 1) to improve equipment and locomotives; 2) to reduce the percentage of out of order equipment; 3) to urge more prompt loading and unloading of freight cars; and 4) to increase car usage by heavier loading and greater daily mileage for each freight car. Relative success was made with each objective. By 1930 the railroad industry had spent close to $7 billion on improvements, including $765 million on locomotives, over $1 billion on freight cars, $398 million on passenger cars and $1 billion on improved roadbed and track.

Obviously, spending was cut back during the Depression years; however, the push for improved efficiency continued. In the years between 1921 and 1941, miles per day run by freight cars improved by 69 percent, the average daily ton-miles per frieght car increased by 77 percent, and the net ton-miles per freight train hour rose by an amazing 99 percent.

Innovations

Early in the twentieth century the railroads sought to improve service by introducing more frequent and faster trains. Somewhat reluctantly, the railroad industry began to look for faster alternatives to the traditional steam locomotive. As early as 1898 the Burlington had experimented with gasoline power, and in 1922 began to use self-propelled rail cars powered by gasoline. Inspired by Burlington's successful venture with gasoline-powered engines, Union Pacific introduced these 'doodlebugs' for branch line passenger service. The railroads continued to explore other forms of motive power, but its first attempts with diesel power were unsuccessful. The General Electric Company solved the problem by using a diesel engine to run electric generators,

Above right: **The years prior to World War II saw steam engines such as this 0-6-0 switcher make way for faster, more economical diesel engines. The** *City of San Francisco (below)* **and the** *City of Portland (below right)* **are two examples of trains powered by this swift new breed.**

Below: The best of two worlds—the 8444 *(right),* the last and perhaps fastest steam engine purchased by the Union Pacific, and the powerful diesel 903 *(left).*

Above: The *City of San Francisco* at the Oakland Pier, circa 1938, and a close-up of the same *(at right).* The train was jointly operated by the Union Pacific, the Southern Pacific and the Chicago & Northwestern.

which in turn ran electric traction motors located in the trucks of the locomotive. A number of lines soon saw the advantages of diesel power over the older steam engines.

Although the diesel, at $100,000 to $200,000 each, was not inexpensive, low operating and maintenance costs made diesels very attractive to many railroads. Diesels require about a quarter of the man-hours for maintenance as steamers because they do not need extensive daily servicing and attention to the firebox and boiler that is necessary with a steam engine. The diesel engine can achieve full power very quickly from a cold engine, whereas a steam locomotive needs a minimum of an hour or two of 'firing up' time.

Diesel power was used first for passenger service. In 1933 Union Pacific announced it would revolutionize passenger service with its new high-speed, three-car streamliner. Produced from a new aluminum alloy and utilizing the latest technology from the auto and aircraft industries, the new car—the M-10000—would weigh only 80 tons. Manufactured by General Motors, this two-cycle eight-cylinder diesel engine was unique in that its use of alloys permitted an incredible weight-to-power ratio of only twenty pounds per horsepower. The first car of this type, christened the *City of Salina,* began daily operations between Kansas City and Salina, Kansas on 31 January 1935. Able to travel at 110 miles per hour, this streamliner was powered with a Winton V-12 600 horsepower distillate motor.

Handling UP's Chicago-Los Angeles service was the *City of Los Angeles.* Consisting of two diesel electric locomotives, four Pullman sleeping cars, a coach and a combination coach-buffet, diner-lounge, mail-baggage, and baggage-dormitory-kitchen car, this train was designed to be the ultimate in travel by rail. The four sleeping cars provided a range of accommodations, from open sections with upper and lower berths to semi-closed sections, bedrooms and compartments. The dining cars used fine china and linens and also were equipped with radios and magazines. As an extra feature, the *Little Nugget* lounge car reproduced the atmosphere of the Gay Nineties. In contrast to the early days of UP, the cross-country trip was made in the comfort of richly appointed and air conditioned cars.

Starting as a once a week, diesel-hauled, 11-car train in 1936, business was so good that a 17-car train had to be added almost immediately. By 1941 the frequency of the service had increased to every third day. After the war, the locomotives and cars were decorated in Union Pacific's golden yellow and grey colors. In addition to the *City of Los Angeles,* UP ran the *City of San Francisco* and the *City of Portland,* each serving the city of its name.

In 1941 diesel power was introduced for freight service and railroad managers soon discovered that diesel motive power could haul freight more efficiently than a steam locomotive could. Three freight cars powered by a diesel can do the work of four cars behind a steamer. The diesel's high horsepower at low speeds allows faster starts and improved schedules, and its low center of gravity permits faster speeds on curves. In addition, the lack of reciprocating parts in the diesel tends to reduce stresses set up in the track by the steam locomotive. Of considerable benefit, a diesel can reverse its motors to add braking power on steep downgrades.

World War II and Beyond

In December of 1941 America became embroiled in the global conflict it had tried desperately to ignore for two years. The Great Depression of the 1930s had consumed the jobs and the savings of an entire generation. Long before the war President Franklin Delano Roosevelt had taken measures to make the most of the railroads during a national emergency. President Roosevelt signed two Emergency Railroad Transportation Acts, one in June 1933 and another on 18 September 1940. In May of 1940 he appointed Ralph Budd as Transportation Commissioner of the Advisory Commission to the Council on National Defense. It was Budd who in the mid-1930s introduced streamlined diesel passenger trains on the Burlington Railroad. He also recognized that railroads wanted to avoid the extent of government control they had known during World War I. On 18 December 1941 President Roosevelt created the Office of Defense Transportation (ODT), headed by Joseph B Eastman, to coordinate all the transportation systems of the nation.

Of major concern to Eastman was the substantial decline in equipment and personnel in the years following World War I. The railroad industry in 1944 had 31 percent fewer locomotives, 24 percent fewer freight cars and 35 percent fewer passenger cars than it did in 1917. In addition, the number of railroad workers had declined nearly 27 percent during the same period. However, the capacity of the freight cars had increased; therefore, the aggregate capacity of the 1.7 million freight cars in 1942 was not noticeably less than all the cars in 1917. In contrast to 1917, traffic moved efficiently. During each of the war years 1942-1945, freight ton-mileage showed a 50 percent increase over railroad freight ton-mileage in 1918. In 1944, freight traffic more than tripled that of 1932. Unlike World War I, World War II became a 'two-front' conflict and rail traffic was flowing in both directions, eliminating the pile up of empty cars at port. Again, labor called for wage increases.

During the war years, the railroads did not pay high dividends, but they did reduce their debts. The railroad industry paid out a considerable amount in tax contributions during this time—over $3 million a day from 1942-1945. On the other hand, during World War I, when the railroads were under government control, operating costs to taxpayers amounted to $2 million a day.

The railroad industry played an essential role in the World War II victory, and was to be equally effective during the Korean conflict.

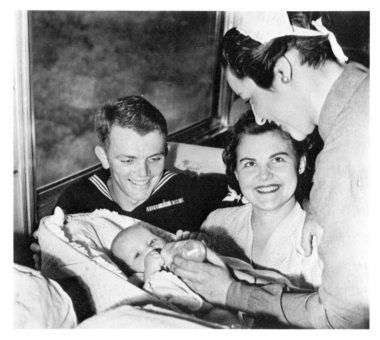

Contributing to the WW II era traffic tonnage were servicemen (and their families) such as is seen *above*. *Below:* President Roosevelt contemplates the role of industry in WW II. By transporting supplies, freight locomotives like this 4-6-6-4 steam engine *(right)* assisted the war effort.

Locomotives

Built for and used only on the Union Pacific, the Big Boy 4-8-8-4 articulated locomotive was the world's most powerful steam locomotive in 1941. Among the largest ever made, the enormous engines were 132 feet long and weighed 1.2 million pounds—over 550 tons. Built to haul 3500-ton loads up steep mountain grades, each locomotive could speed up to 80 miles per hour on level track. Under full steam, Big Boy consumed 22 tons of coal and 22,000 gallons of water in an hour. The 14 wheel tender had a capacity of 25,000 gallons of water and a coal capacity of 28 tons. Rarely used on passenger trains, Big Boy locomotives contributed to America's victory during World War II by hauling millions of tons of supplies to seaports on both coasts.

Union Pacific 4-6-6-4 Number 3985, the *Challenger*, was built by American Locomotive Company. Second in size only to the Big Boys, it was the fastest and most versatile freight locomotive owned by the railroad. The largest steam locomotive yet restored, the *Challenger* is on display at the California Railroad Museum.

Left, at top: **This 4-12-2 Union Pacific-type locomotive is prime evidence of the UP's pioneering spirit. The 4-6-6-4 Challenger-type** *(left)* **was the next design step after the 4-12-2.** *Below:* **The Union Passenger Station in El Paso in the early 1950s.** *At right:* **A Big Boy-type locomotive, one of the largest and most powerful steam locomotives in the world.**

The 844 was placed in service in 1944, a 4-8-4 northern-type engine with a 14-wheeled tender and a water capacity of 23,500 gallons. It was the last steam locomotive purchased by Union Pacific. Known for their speed, UP's 4-8-4s pulled such famous passenger trains as the *Overland Limited, Los Angeles Limited, Pacific Limited, Portland Rose* and *Challenger* passenger trains on portions of their runs between Omaha, the West Coast and the Pacific Northwest. Between 1957 and 1959, old number 844 handled freight trains in Nebraska. Renumbered 8444 in 1962 to distinguish her from a diesel freight locomotive that was numbered 844, 8444 is used today as UP's ambassador to numerous civic celebrations.

The Electro-Motive Division (EMD) of General Electric was responsible for many of the diesel locomotives in operation after World War II. Sleek units, considered among the most graceful looking locomotives in American railroading, they evolved from the first Union Pacific diesel locomotives of 1934. The 'E' series was started by EMD in the late 1930s. Delivery of the E-8s, virtually identical to the E-9s, in the 1950s completed dieselization of Union Pacific's passenger service. In 1955 EMD E-9 Number 951 was the last high-speed diesel electric built for service on UP's famous streamliner and domeliner passenger trains. She was a 2400 horsepower locomotive and had pulled such famous trains as the *City of Los Angeles, City of Portland, City of San Francisco, City of St Louis* and *Challenger*.

'Centennial' locomotives were introduced by UP from April of 1969 to September of 1971 to commemorate the 100th anniversary of the historic driving of the golden spike at Promontory in 1869. The 6900 series Centennial diesels

At left: An advertisement for a UP excursion to three US national parks. *Below:* A lone UP diesel crosses Montana. *At bottom:* A UP freight train journeys across the country. *Opposite above:* UP Number 8444 makes its way through the rugged terrain of the western United States. *Opposite below:* A UP EMD SD-60. Many of the UP's diesel engines were produced by EMD—the Electro-Motive Division of General Electric.

Because just riding Union Pacific's Domeliners to and from Chicago, Kansas City or St. Louis is an extra two day vacation — restful and thoroughly enjoyable.

Next trip, try it yourself. Take the time to relax and unwind. For business or vacation travelers arriving refreshed, ready for work or play, is a good investment.

Spacious Pullman rooms provide complete privacy

when you want it or you may join congenial groups in the Lounge or Dome cars. Mealtimes are happy events in both the Diner or the exclusive Dome Dining Car.

Family Fares apply to husband and wife traveling together or when one or both parents accompany the children.

Low Coach Fares provide savings, your own reserved seat, access to the Dome Coach, Lounge and Dining Cars. Generous baggage allowance on all tickets.

UNION PACIFIC RAILROAD

Early Reservations are advisable. Call any Union Pacific office.

OMAHA 2, NEBRASKA

Short Lesson in Anatomy

(FOR **EVERYONE** WHO TRAVELS)

Head. Your head isn't filled with worries about the weather when you go Pullman. That's because you know—rain, sleet, or snow—you're safer in a Pullman than you are in your own home.

Finger. The only finger you lift when you go Pullman is the one you use to press the buzzer that summons the porter. You can ask him to run errands, get things for you, perform many other special services.

Legs. Very handy things, legs, aboard a Pullman. You can use them for walking around, visiting different parts of your world on wheels. You can also use them at night for stretching out full length on your soft Pullman bed.

Smile. You wear the biggest smile you own when you get there by Pullman. You arrive on time right in the heart of town—relaxed, refreshed, ready for business or pleasure.

Go Pullman

COMFORTABLE, DEPENDABLE, AND—ABOVE ALL—SAFE!

had 6600 horsepower engines, making them the most powerful diesel electric locomotives ever built, weighing 540,000 lbs, 98 feet 5 inches long. Preserved in parks and museums, 6936 remain in excursion service for UP. In 1971 6946 EMD DDA40X was the last of the 'double-diesel' super-powered locomotives built for UP. Their unique combination of cowl-unit cab with DD-type car body is unmistakable. Internally, the units employed modular electrical controls that later became standard on the Dash 2 line. They have two 6600 horsepower 16-cylinder engines.

The Decline in Passenger Service

The years following World War II saw the continued decline of railroad passenger service as Americans turned to autos, buses and planes. Railroad passenger trains were viewed more and more as emergency transportation in case of blizzards or airline strikes. Numerous reasons contributed to this decline, including labor difficulties, government assistance which favored highways and airlines over railroads, railroad management indifferent to the needs of the travelers and public relations problems. Railroads, which once controlled the monopoly on intercity traffic, dropped down to 37 percent of all intercity traffic during 1920-1970. Airlines, buses and the private automobile controlled the remaining 63 percent. In 1970 railroad passenger traffic dropped to a meager seven percent of all commercial transportation. Leading the public carrier market were the airlines, with 73 percent; ranking second were buses, with nearly 16 percent; and of course private autos also accounted for the loss in passenger traffic. Clearly, the time had come for drastic measures. Railroads determined that their best market was freight. Consequently, the passage of the

Far left: A UP ad promoting the smooth ride of its domeliners. Domeliners featured Pullman sleepers—described in the ad at left. Below left: A UP 2419 GE C30-7 leads a train through the coal country of Wyoming. Below: Service with a view on Amtrak.

National Rail Passenger Service Act in 1970 transferred all passenger carrier service to 'Amtrak,' for America, Travel and Track. This national rail passenger system had three goals: to improve employee courtesy and service to the public; to offer reliable performance and better-maintained equipment; and to issue accurate information to travelers.

Railroad Revitalization

After a rash of bankruptcies among railroad companies in the early seventies attracted national attention, the Railroad Revitalization and Regulatory Reform Act of April 1976, known as the 4R Act, amended the Rail Reorganization Act of December 1973 and set the railroad industry back on its feet. It revolutionized the government's approach to the nation's freight-hauling railroads, called for a restructuring of bankrupt lines, and made available $2.1 billion in repayable financing to help with the 10-year rehabilitation plans of six railroads in the Northeast and parts of the Midwest. The 4R Act also called for modernization of passenger service, which was badly needed, and authorized Amtrak to upgrade and operate trackage in the Washington-New York-Boston corridor. When Amtrak began running in 1971 it was almost totally dependent on existing private railroads for equipment and facilities for the first two years. By 1983 Amtrak was the only intercity rail passenger carrier in the United States and is today the nation's sixth largest public carrier in number of passengers carried.

The Staggers Rail Act, passed in 1980 by President Jimmy Carter, substantially loosened the federal restraints on the railroad industry that had existed since 1887. Its sweeping reforms had an impact similar to that of the Transportation Act of 1920. Although it was short of total deregulation, the Act allowed for more free market competition among railroads and retained ICC jurisdiction in ratemaking only over those railroads with 'market dominance.'

Mergers and Consolidations

Railroad history cannot ignore the impact of mergers and consolidations on the development of American railroads. As early as 1880 mergers were accepted as common business practice. In the twentieth century railroads are still combining and separating. The Union Pacific is no exception. Strengthening its system and consolidating its influence across the country, the Union Pacific acquired the Missouri Pacific—aka Mo-Pac—and the Western Pacific on 22 December 1981.

The Missouri Pacific

The Missouri Pacific Railroad can trace its origins back to the Iron Mountain route in Missouri, for which the first tracks were laid in 1853. At the same time, other railroad projects that would later become part of the Missouri Pacific were beginning in Missouri and Texas.

In 1879 Jay Gould became president of the company when he purchased controlling interest of the Missouri Pacific. Using Mo-Pac as the foundation, Gould created a network of rail lines in the South and Southwest. Within the next year, five other western railroads would become part of the Missouri Pacific. In 1885 Gould lost control of the Texas & Pacific, and in 1888, of the Missouri-Kansas-Texas Railroad. By this time, only the Iron Mountain still remained under his control.

However, between 1885 and 1892, Missouri Pacific mileage increased through construction of subsidiary lines, including extensions to Colorado and Louisiana. When Jay Gould died in December of 1892, control of the company passed to his son, George J Gould, and many other smaller subsidiaries would merge with the company between 1909 and 1923.

The years of the Great Depression would be difficult for the Missouri Pacific. The company was placed in receivership for 23 years. After its reorganization, Mo-Pac vigorously went after new business. It modernized its equipment, constructed new classification yards and became the first railroad to acquire a solid state computer. Expansion by acquisition was the rule through the late 1960s. In 1980 stockholders voted to merge with the Union Pacific Corporation.

Right: This General Motors ad proudly features a Western Pacific diesel freight locomotive. **Far right:** A UP quadruple header crosses a trestle near Keddie, California. The Union Pacific finally gained access to this route when it acquired the Western Pacific in 1981.

The Western Pacific

In 1900 the Gould network of railroads (including Western Maryland, Wabash, Missouri Pacific, and Denver & Rio Grande) spanned most of the continent from Baltimore, Maryland to Ogden, Utah, with only a short gap in Pennsylvania. The Southern Pacific connection at Ogden gave the system considerable traffic, but that connection was lost when EH Harriman took control of Union Pacific and Southern Pacific, shutting out Denver & Rio Grande from Ogden—and therefore the West. Harriman had gained control of the Southern Pacific by purchasing Collis

A NEW DAY DAWNS IN RAILROADING

War traffic has more than doubled the volume of freight hauled by the Western Pacific Railroad from Salt Lake City to San Francisco. Wherever the going is toughest on this rugged route, General Motors Diesel freight locomotives have kept this vast stream of vital munitions moving steadily.

A crack "Express Train" of 1865 as pictured by Currier & Ives. Four years later an important new era began when the first railroad linked the Atlantic and Pacific.

AMERICAN EXPRESS TRAIN.

Throughout history, wars have set up new milestones of transportation progress. And with this war, it is the General Motors Diesel Locomotive that is ushering in the new era. What advances the future will bring are already apparent in the present performance of these locomotives and the way they are helping to meet the abnormal demands upon the railroads today.

KEEP AMERICA STRONG · BUY MORE BONDS

War building is being rushed ahead with reliable General Motors Diesel power. In the days to come this dependable, economical power will be ready to do the hard jobs of peace.

GM GENERAL MOTORS **DIESEL POWER**

LOCOMOTIVES.....................ELECTRO-MOTIVE DIVISION, La Grange, Ill.

ENGINES..150 to 2000 H.P...CLEVELAND DIESEL ENGINE DIVISION, Cleveland, Ohio

ENGINES.....15 to 250 H.P......DETROIT DIESEL ENGINE DIVISION, Detroit, Mich.

Huntington's holdings in the Southern Pacific and Central Pacific following Huntington's death in 1900. Southern Pacific, in effect, had a monopoly over the area. A link to the West was clearly a necessity for the Gould system. In answer to this need, George Gould, son and successor of Jay Gould, organized the Western Pacific Railway to run from San Francisco, California through the canyons of the Feather River and Beckwourth Pass to Salt Lake City, Utah. The railroad would, in turn, connect with the Rio Grande-Missouri Pacific system.

In 1906 the first spike was driven at Oakland, California. Three years later, on 1 November 1909, the road was completed on a trestle across the Spanish Creek near Keddie, California as track gangs from the east and west met. The final spike would be driven with considerable less fanfare than that historic moment 40 years earlier at Promontory. There would be no cheering crowds or flowing champagne—only a few housewives and their children gathered as an Italian trackman drove home the last iron spike.

Freight service began in January of 1910, with passenger service starting in August. Because the railroad had no branches to feed it, revenue didn't cover operating expenses. In 1915 Rio Grande defaulted on its obligations and Western Pacific went into receivership. A year later Gould lost control when the company was reorganized as the Western Pacific Railroad.

In 1917 the Western Pacific gained control of the Tidewater Southern, an interurban that provided access to Reno, Nevada via Stockton, California and the southern end of the Nevada-California-Oregon road.

Arthur Curtiss James acquired control of the company in 1926 and during the late 1920s and early 30s, the company acquired and constructed new lines, but would again be placed in receivership during the Depression. Western Pacific was reorganized in 1945, following a lengthy court battle.

Following World War II, Western Pacific was able to carry out the long-held dream of operating a route between Chicago, Illinois and Oakland, California. In conjunction with Rio Grande and the Burlington, Western Pacific began running the *California Zephyr*, the first long distance train to carry Vista-Domes. Because of the *Zephyr's* routing, it was not as fast as the Union Pacific's *City of Francisco*, but the *Zephyr's* route was designed to take full advantage of the view of the spectacular Feather River Canyon and the Sierra Nevadas. The *California Zephyr* was quite a success and operated until 21 March 1970.

Southern Pacific and Santa Fe attempted to purchase the company in 1960, but the Interstate Commerce Commission rejected their bids. Twenty years later Western Pacific was acquired by Union Pacific, giving UP the link to San Francisco it had surveyed years before. WP was absorbed into the Union Pacific system and became known as the Fourth Operating Division of UP. In 1985, in response to employee pressure, it was renamed the Feather River Division, and thereby regained a sense of its old identity.

The Missouri-Kansas-Texas Railroad

Union Pacific's most recent merger to date is with the Missouri-Kansas-Texas Railroad, the KT line, or simply 'Katy.' The Katy originated as the Union Pacific Southern Branch (no relation to the Union Pacific). Organizers wanted to build a line from the Port of New Orleans to the northern Kansas border. Supported with government land grants, construction began in 1869, reached the southern Kansas border and then extended into Oklahoma. Through acquisitions, it gained lines in Missouri and Texas and its name was changed to the Missouri-Kansas-Texas Railroad. In 1873 Jay Gould acquired control and added more lines, but he later lost contol when several midwestern railroads went bankrupt. The railroad remained in control of creditors until 1910.

Like many other railroads of the time, the KMT entered a period of decline following World War II. Unable to compete with long-haul trucks and other railroads, the Katy declared bankruptcy in the 1950s. The railroad enjoyed profitability in the 1970s, but has struggled in recent years in the wake of deregulation.

Today Katy operates primarily between the Gulf Coast at Galveston and Omaha/Council Bluffs. UP executives have long considered the Katy a vital part of the Union Pacific's

Worth looking into... TRAVEL ON THE Domeliners

Dome Dining Room

Charcoal Grill

Salad Bar

Gold Room private dining

Picture Window Dining Room

Only on Union Pacific can you enjoy the thrilling experience of dining in a dome car. When arranging a trip to or from the Pacific Coast, ask for reservations on a Union Pacific Domeliner, Pullmans and Coaches.

Union Pacific DOMELINERS

"CITY OF LOS ANGELES"
(Between Chicago-Los Angeles)

"CITY OF PORTLAND"
(Between Chicago-Portland-Tacoma-Seattle)

main route between Kansas and Texas because of trackage rights agreements. Because severe financial difficulties now plague the Katy and her sound welfare has always been vital to UP and the shippers in the Katy service area, UP filed application with the ICC to merge with the Katy. The ICC approved the merger on 13 May 1988 and UP assumed control on 12 August 1988. The merger will guarantee the preservation of key routes between the Midwest and the Gulf of Mexico.

Below: Western Pacific took its identity, as well as its logo, from the Feather River region. Advertisements for Union Pacific domeliners *(below left)*, UP's affordable *Challenger* domeliner *(at bottom)* and Western Pacific's *California Zephyr (right)*, complete with Vista-Dome cars.

"The CHALLENGER"
All Coach Domeliner
FAST, CONVENIENT SERVICE
BETWEEN CHICAGO AND
Los Angeles

Look at those comfortable Coach slumber-seats with backs easily adjustable to a reclining position . . . and stretch-out leg rests. Yes, you get complete relaxation, at low cost, on "The Challenger" Domeliner.

Then there's the Astra Dome where you can enjoy an eye-level view of the passing panorama. No additional charge.

If you prefer to go Pullman, we suggest the "City of Los Angeles" Domeliner featuring an Astra Dome dining car and Astra Dome lounge.

In either case, going Coach or Pullman, it's much more restful and enjoyable than driving mile after mile on crowded highways under a hot summer sun.

FAMILY TRAVEL PLAN
—an ideal, money-saving plan for two or more persons. Only one adult pays the full fare. For others in the family group, there's a big reduction in rail fare. Ask at your nearest ticket or travel office. You'll be amazed at how little it costs to travel in comfort.

NOTE: On arrival you can rent a car for visiting or sightseeing. Hertz Rent-a-Car service is convenient and economical.

MAIL COUPON FOR FREE FOLDER

UNION PACIFIC RAILROAD
Room 775, Omaha 2, Nebr.

Please send full information about your Domeliner service to California.

Name_____
Address_____
City_____Zone___State____
Phone No._____
I am interested in your All-Expense tours to California. ☐

UNION PACIFIC RAILROAD

look **up...**
look **down...**
look
all around!

EXTRA COMFORT
EXTRA PLEASURE
no extra fare!

RIDE THE VISTA-DOME
California Zephyr

CHICAGO · DENVER · SALT LAKE CITY · SAN FRANCISCO

Aboard the only transcontinental train with Vista-Dome cars you enjoy a panoramic view of magnificent mountain scenery! Travel through the snow-capped Colorado Rockies and California's Feather River Canyon during daylight hours!

Vista-Domes for all passengers. Private rooms, lowers, uppers and reserved reclining coach seats. Through sleeping cars daily, between New York and San Francisco.

Make reservations at any railroad ticket office or travel bureau.

The most talked-about train in the country

Roomy, restful coaches

Five Vista-Dome cars

Two beautiful lounge cars

Luxurious private rooms

Include Southern California

via San Francisco
without extra rail fare

BURLINGTON	RIO GRANDE	WESTERN PACIFIC
A. Cotsworth, Jr. Passenger Traffic Mgr. Chicago, Illinois	H. F. Eno Passenger Traffic Mgr. Denver, Colorado	Jos. G. Wheeler Passenger Traffic Mgr. San Francisco, Calif.

The Union Pacific and the Railroad Industry Today

In the 1960s it became evident that passenger service was on the decline and freight held the most promise for the Union Pacific. Quicker classification and switching of freight cars naturally helped speed up freight operations. Longer hauls and a drop in less-than-carload freight traffic, as well as faster average speeds (20 miles per hour), improved the financial position of the rail industry. The introduction of piggy-back service after World War I spread throughout the industry, and by 1965 this economical transportation of loaded highway truck-trailers on railway flatcars was producing almost four percent of all freight carloadings.

Faster freight movement was made possible in part by a new system of Centralized Traffic Control (CTC), improvements in roadbeds and the conversion to continuous welded rails. CTC is the method of regulating over-the-road train movements from a distant point with electronic equipment to keep trains moving and reduce delays. Under direct CTC operation all switches are remote controlled by a dispatcher in a control center. The CTC board is a miniaturized duplicate layout of an actual section of main line track. Sidings, spurs, switches, block signals, hot box detectors, rock slide fence installations, grades and miles between sidings are all depicted on the board. The board is also equipped with microwave radio to keep the dispatcher in voice contact with the engine and caboose crews of each train operating on the particular section of the line controlled by the board. This 'push button' railroading is one of the great improvements in safety and efficiency since the air brake, the automatic coupler and automatic block signals.

The Union Pacific Corporation

A holding and managing company for Missouri Pacific, Union Pacific and Western Pacific, under the name Pacific Rail Systems, Inc, operates as a wholly owned subsidiary of Union Pacific Corporation. Their three traffic departments have been merged to allow for a uniform operating and pricing policy. As of 1984, their combined systems support 1742 locomotives, 67,778 freight cars, and operate 1432 miles of trackage.

Today the Union Pacific Corporation maintains the nation's third largest railroad system. Comprised of the Union Pacific Railroad, the Missouri Pacific, the Western Pacific, and the Katy, its total trackage measures over 23,000 miles and extends to 10 of the nation's 20 largest ports and all of the major Midwestern gateways. The Union Pacific System serves 4,000 communities in 21 states, shipping agricultural and industrial products to domestic and foreign markets.

Employing over 30,000 men and women throughout the nation, the Union Pacific Railroad remains Nebraska's

Below: **The UP refinery at Long Beach, California.** *At right:* **UP 6946, with 6600 hp and 32 cylinders, was one of the most powerful diesel engines ever built. Built by EMD and designated DDA40X, the 6900 series Centennial diesels were introduced in 1969 to commemorate the 100th anniversary of the driving of the golden spike.**

largest private employer with 5494 employees. It is also the largest private employer in Wyoming with 1486 employees. Wage impact in the Union Pacific System states increases significantly when these dollars circulate within a community. The largest impact is evident in the Omaha-Council Bluffs area, where total wages exceeded $173 million in 1987. The UP Railroad alone had a total dollar impact of $2,080,533,395 on the nation's economy in 1987.

In addition to the railroad, the Union Pacific Corporation consists of five operating companies engaged in activities vital to the national economy: transportation, energy, natural resources, hazardous waste management, computer logistical systems and real estate development.

Overnight Transportation, one of the country's largest general freight trucking companies, serves 39 states through 128 terminals. Overnight specializes in less-than-truckload shipments, transporting a variety of products, including paper, textiles and food products. Due to intense industry-wide price competition in 1987, Overnight experienced a financially disappointing year; however, by the second quarter of 1988 Overnight cleared $15 million and executives expect continued success with their fully integrated transportation system.

Union Pacific Resources, a consolidation of Champlin Petroleum and Rocky Mountain Energy, consists of integrated oil and gas operations, which explore for, develop and produce crude oil and natural gas, and manufacture and market petroleum products; and a mining operation that develops soda ash, coal and other minerals. In its second quarter of 1988, UP Resources are well over the $104 million mark.

United States Pollution Control, Inc, which Union Pacific acquired in the first quarter of 1988, provides comprehensive hazardous waste management services to industrial customers and government through its Treatment & Recovery, Disposal, Analytical Services and Research and Development divisions. By its second quarter, USPC surpassed $2 million in net income.

Union Pacific Technologies, formed in May of 1987, develops and markets high-tech computer and communications systems and services. It provides computer and communications support to the corporation and markets logistical services to other shippers and carriers. Its financial report is not distinguished from the Union Pacific Corporate record.

Union Pacific Realty develops individual sites and buildings, including offices, hotels, and research and development facilities, along with business and industrial parks, on its 21,000 acres of prime real estate in major metropolitan centers. Its financial status as of the second quarter of the 1988 fiscal year is at $13 million.

The June 1988 issue of the *Union Pacific Railroad Info Magazine* highlights a 10 percent increase in the first five months of 1988 over 1987 results. Coal traffic was up nine percent over the first five months of 1987, while chemical carloadings were up 10 percent; grain 17 percent; and intermodal, three percent. Metals and ores jumped 58 percent. Steel in all its forms—plate, slabs, coiled, sheet, pipe, structurals and recyclable—account for the largest portion of UP's volume in metals and ores.

Technological Improvements in the 1980s

The Union Pacific Corporation is constantly updating its procedures and pursuing innovative technologies in order to produce results more efficiently and at lower manufacturing costs. A customer service telephone line is located in St Louis, and Union Pacific offers a software package to shippers that enables them to trace their own cars.

A three-level Shipment Monitoring System designed by UP Technologies offers unique features to shippers. Level one involves tracking shipments across multiple carriers and modes. Level two includes analysis of shipments in progress and notification of transit exceptions as compared to predefined performance standards. At level three, UP Technologies provides pro-active handling of jeopardized shipments.

TeleTrans, UP's new automated car tracing and notification system, introduced in April of 1988, is a voice

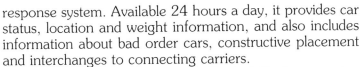

response system. Available 24 hours a day, it provides car status, location and weight information, and also includes information about bad order cars, constructive placement and interchanges to connecting carriers.

A system-wide Transportation Control Center, covering the Railroad's entire 20-state network, is scheduled to begin operation in Omaha by early 1989. This facility will include a locomotive distribution, train management and train dispatching center. It will handle the work of eight widely-dispersed dispatching centers—from Spring, Texas to Portland, Oregon—monitoring up to 700 trains a day.

Judging from these advances in communication technology, the Union Pacific is looking toward future shipping efficiency and growth. Employing bright, creative men and women, the Union Pacific Corporation will continue to excell in overall performance with the help and professional guidance of its management and through the dedication and commitment of its employees and their families. What began as a vision to span the continent in the 1850s has evolved into an innovative, diversified company of the 1980s.

Far left: **UP 164 pulls into the refinery. The Union Pacific today—***(above left)* **a hopper car loaded with grain;** *(above right)* **a chemist at the USPCI lab;** *(below left)* **planners at UP Technologies at work on a logistical program; and** *(below right)* **an Overnite truck.** *Overleaf:* **Representing the consolidated UP—Missouri Pacific 9019 and Union Pacific 3257 are ready to roll into the future.**

Index

Adams, Charles: 80, 83, 84, 87
Adamson Act: 96
Air brake: 66
Ames Monument: *60*
Ames, Oakes: 60, 72
Ames, Oliver: 58, 60, 72
Amtrak: 115
Atchison, Topeka & Santa Fe RR: 10
Atlantic & Pacific RR: 10
Automatic block signal: 66
Automatic coupler: 66
Baltimore & Ohio RR: 8, 96
Beckwith and Quinn: 87
Benton, Thomas H: 23
Berry, JB: 61
Big Four: 8, *10*, 12, 88
Buchanan, President James: 23
Budd, Ralph: 108
Buffalo Trail: 23
Burch, John: 8
Burlington RR: 72, 96, 102, 108
California & Oregon RR: 10
California Zephyr: 118
Camden & Amboy RR: 66
Canadian Pacific Railway: 61
Carnegie, Andrew: 66
Casement, Dan: 48, 52
Casement, Jack: 13, 48, 52
Cattle industry: 64
Central Pacific RR: 8, 10, 12, 16, 18, 43, 48, 50, 52, 61, 88, 92, 96
Centralized Traffic Control (CTC): 120
Challenger: 110, *110*, 112
Chase, Senator Salmon P: 18
Chesapeake & Ohio RR: 96
Chicago & Alton RR: 91
Chicago & Northwestern RR: 16, 18, 96
Cisco, JJ: 26
City of Los Angeles: 106, 112
City of Portland: 103, 106, 112
City of San Francisco: 102, 106, 112, 118
City of St Louis: 112
City of Salina: 106
Clark, William A: 88
Cleveland, President Grover: 78
Cooke, Jay: 71
Council Bluffs, Iowa: 20, 21, 23, 24, 32, 43, 55, 56
Cow towns: 64, *64*
Credit Mobilier: 46, 58
Crocker, Charles: 8, 10, *10*, 12, 50
Curtis, Samuel R: 23
Cushing Caleb: 8
Denver & Rio Grande RR: 116
Denver Pacific RR: 72
Dey, Peter A: 10, 13, 18, 23, 26, 29, 37, 58, 62
Diesel power: 102, 106
Dillon, Sydney: 58, 72
Dix, General John A: 12, 26
Dodge, Major General Grenville M: 6, *6*, 12, 13, 26, 58, 61, 72, 74, 83
Doodlebugs: 102

Duff, John R: 50
Durant, Thomas C: 8-10, 12, 16, 20, 21, 23, 26, 50, 52, 58, 62
Eastman, Joseph B: 108
Eddy, JM: 38, 39
Electro-Motive Division of General Electric: 112
Elkins Act: 78
Emergency Railroad Transportation Acts: 108
Erie Canal: 8
Erie RR: 96
Evans, James A: 46, 54
Farnam, Henry: 8, 9, *18*, 20, 2, 62
Fillmore, President Millard: 10
Ford, Henry: 100
General, The: 11
General Electric Company: 102
General Sherman, The: 70, *70*
Golden Spike Ceremony: *12, 13, 16, 17, 50, 52-53,* 70, *128*
Gould, George J: 78, 96, 116, 118
Gould, Jay: 71, 72, *72,* 74, 78, 80, 84
Granger laws: 78
Grant, General Ulysses S: 24, 30, 34, *34,* 45, 47, 48, 52, 58, 60, 74
Great Depression: 102, 108, 116
Great Dining Car War of 1888-89: 83
Great Northern RR: 96
Hanna, Mark: 84
Harlan, James: 23, 56
Harriman, Edward H: 61, 72, 88, 89, 90, 91, 96, 116
Harrison, President Benjamin: 66, 79
Hepburn Act: 78, 79
Hill, Jim: 71, 90, 96
Hopkins, Mark: 8, 10, *10,* 12, 50
'Hotel Train': 66
Hoxie, HM: 48, 54
Huntington, Collis P: 8, 10, *10,* 12, 50, 88
Hurd, MF: 54
Illinois Central RR: 10, 88, 91
Interstate Commerce Commission: 78, 79, 90, 96, 98, 115, 118, 119
Iron Mountain RR: 116
Janney, Major Eli H: 66
Judah, Theodore D: 6, *6,* 8
Jupiter: 13, *53,* 70, *76-77*
Kansas Central RR: 75
Kansas Pacific RR: 12, 16, 72, 75, 78
Lincoln, Abraham: 10, *10,* 23, 24
Locomotives:
American-type engine: 67, 70, see also 4-4-0
Big Boy : *47,* 110, *111*
Camel 768: 70
'Dirt Burner' locomotive: 67
EMD 'E' series: 112
EMD SD-60: 113
M-10000: 106
Number 1: See *The General Sherman*
Number 5: 24
Number 23: 24
Number 119: 13, *53,* 70, *76-77*
Number 164: *122*
Number 844: See Number 8444
Number 3985: 43
Number 4466: *1, 97*
Number 6018: *2-3*

Number 8444: *43, 63,* 104, *112, 113, 127*
UP 2419 GE C30-7: 115
UP 3257: *124-25*
UP 6946: *121*
'Wooten' locomotive: 67
0-4-0 Pony: *34-35*
2-8-2 Number 1938: *71*
4-4-0 Camel: *39,* 47
4-12-2 Union Pacific-type: *110*
6900 series Centennial diesels: 112
Los Angeles Limited: 88, 112
Mississippi & Missouri RR: 10, 18, 55, 56
Missouri-Kansas-Texas RR (KATY): 72, 116, 118, 120
Missouri Pacific RR: 16, 72, 78, 96, 116, 120
Missouri Pacific 9019: 124-25
Mobile & Ohio RR: 10
Model T: 100
Montague, Samuel: 13, *13,* 50
Moore, William H: 96
Morgan, JP: 90, 92, 96
McAdoo, William G: 98

National Rail Passenger Service Act: 115
New York Central RR: 96
Northern Pacific RR: 10, 96
Northern Securities Company: 90
Northwest Shippers Advisory Board: 100
Northern Railway: 43
Oden, Henry B: 23
Office of Defense (ODT): 108
Olcott, Thomas W: 23
Omaha, Nebraska: 26, 29, 30, 37, 50, *54,* 55, 56, *57,* 72
Overland Flyer: 83
Overland Limited: 112
Overnight Transportation: 122
Pacific Limited: 112
Pacific Pullman Company: 66, 83
Pacific Railroad Act: 10, 12, 23, 24, 43, 58, 70
Panic of 1873: 70, 71, *72*
Panic of 1893: 88
Passenger service: 64, 66, 67, 106, 115
Pennsylvania RR: 96
Perry, Commodore Matthew: 8

Plumbe, John: 18
Poor, Henry V: 23, 26
Portland Rose: 112
Promontory Point, Utah: 44, 48, 50, 64
Pullman, George: 66
Pullman Palace Cars: 66
Pullman Sleeper Cars: *66-67,* 83, *82-83,* 114
Railroad Revitalization and Regulatory Reform Act: 115
Railroad Safety Appliance Act: 66, 79
Railroads' War Board: 96, 98
Rawlins, General John A: 37, 38, 39
Reed, Samuel B: 52, 54, *59*
Rio Grande Western RR: 72
Robinson, William: 66
Rock Island RR: 21, 96
Rock Springs Massacre: 87
Rocket: 8
Rogers Works: 70
Roosevelt, President Franklin: 108, *108*
Roosevelt, President Theodore: 90,

92
San Pedro, Los Angeles & Salt Lake RR: 88
Seymour, Colonel Silas: 29, 46
Sherman Antitrust Act: 90
Sherman, General William Tecumseh: 11, 34, 35, *35,* 45, 47, 48, 49, 52
Shilling, WW: 16
Shipment Monitoring System: 122
Sioux City & Pacific Railway: 12, 16
Southern Pacific RR: 88, 90, 91, 92, 96, 116, 118
Southern RR: 96
Staggers Rail Act: 115
Standard Time Act: 79
Stanford, Leland: 8, 10, *10,* 12, 13, 50
Stephenson, George: 8
TeleTrans: 122
Tennessee Coal & Iron Company: 92
Texas & Pacific RR: 10, 72, 78
Train, George Francis: 58
Transportation Act of 1920: 98,

115
Transportation Control Center: 123
Union Coal Company: 84
Union Pacific Coal Company: 84
Union Pacific Corporation: 120, 122
Union Pacific Depot, Cheyenne: 7
Union Pacific Railroad Company: 12
Union Pacific Railway, Central Branch: 12, 16, 75
Union Pacific Realty: 122
Union Pacific Resources: 122
Union Pacific Technologies: 122
United States Pollution Control, Inc: 122
United Steel Corporation: 92

Vanderbilt, Cornelius: 96
Vista-Domes: 118
Wabash RR: 116
Welch, Asabel: 66
Western & Atlantic RR: 11, 12
Western Maryland RR: 116
Western Pacific RR: 16, 90, 96, 116, 118, 120
Westinghouse, George: 66
Whitney, Asa: 8
Whyte system: 67
Wilson, James F: 72
Wilson, President Woodrow: 96, 98
Winans: Ross: 70
Woodburner: *40-41*
World War I: 96, 108
World War II: 108, 118

Below: **A boy's dream come true—at the throttle of a Union Pacific 8444. Known for its speed, the 8444 pulled such well-known passenger trains as the *Overland Limited, Pacific Limited* and *Portland Rose.* Today, this 4-8-4 engine serves as the UP's roving ambassador.** *Overleaf:* **A reenactment of the meeting of the Union Pacific and Central Pacific at Promontory.**